statements

Also by Amy Borkowsky

Amy's Answering Machine: Messages from Mom

STATEMENTS

True Tales of Life, Love, and Credit Card Bills

Amy Borkowsky

Roadside Amusements

an imprint of

Chamberlain Bros.

a member of Penguin Group (USA) Inc.

New York

2005

ROADSIDE AMUSEMENTS
an imprint of
CHAMBERLAIN BROS.
Published by the Penguin Group
Penguin Group (USA) Inc., 375 Hudson Street, New York, New York 10014, USA
Penguin Group (Canada), 90 Eglinton Avenue East, Suite 700, Toronto, Ontario
M4P 2Y3, Canada (a division of Pearson Penguin Canada Inc.)
Penguin Books Ltd, 80 Strand, London WC2R 0RL, England
Penguin Ireland, 25 St Stephen's Green, Dublin 2, Ireland
(a division of Penguin Books Ltd)
Penguin Group (Australia), 250 Camberwell Road, Camberwell, Victoria 3124, Australia
(a division of Pearson Australia Group Pty Ltd)
Penguin Books India Pvt Ltd, 11 Community Centre, Panchsheel Park,
New Delhi–110 017, India
Penguin Group (NZ), Cnr Airborne and Rosedale Roads, Albany,
Auckland 1310, New Zealand (a division of Pearson New Zealand Ltd)
Penguin Books (South Africa) (Pty) Ltd, 24 Sturdee Avenue, Rosebank,
Johannesburg 2196, South Africa

Penguin Books Ltd, Registered Offices: 80 Strand, London WC2R 0RL, England

Library of Congress Cataloging-in-Publication Data

Borkowsky, Amy.
Statements : true tales of life, love, and credit card bills / Amy Borkowsky.
p.   cm.
ISBN 1-59609-087-1
1. Borkowsky, Amy.   2. American wit and humor.   I. Title.
PN6165.B66   2005   2005045519
818'.602—dc22

Printed in the United States of America
1   3   5   7   9   10   8   6   4   2

Book design by Elke Sigal

While the author has made every effort to provide accurate telephone numbers and
Internet addresses at the time of publication, neither the publisher nor the author
assumes any responsibility for errors, or for changes that occur after publication.
Further, the publisher does not have any control over and does not assume
any responsibility for author or third-party websites or their content.

This book is not authorized, prepared, approved, licensed, or endorsed by
American Express.

Names and identifying characteristics have been changed to protect individuals' privacy.

This book is dedicated to
my accountant, Anthony,
who advised me never to
throw away a credit card bill.

Contents

Introduction

Not long ago, I was looking through some boxes in my closet and became nostalgic. I'm talking all-out, mascara-running, nose-blowing nostalgic.

The boxes didn't hold faded photographs.

They didn't contain love letters.

They held twelve years of credit card statements, chronicling virtually every significant event in my life as a single career woman.

While I was too busy to keep a diary, it turned out that American Express had kept one for me.

They've recorded for all eternity the fact that on July 7, 1992, I spent $89.12 at Victoria's Secret—and that on July 17 I returned the entire purchase, documenting in black-and-white a relationship that unraveled just before The Lingerie Phase. The $30.25 charge for my first caller ID box forever preserves the memory of my fruitless attempts to avoid my interfering mother, and I can tell just how many late nights I worked at my high-pressure ad job by tracking the charges for Chinese takeout.

This is a collection of true stories about how I, literally, *spent* my early years living, working, and looking for love in Manhattan, when it seemed like the only knight in armor I'd find was the one on the front of my Amex card.

I should mention that some names and identifying details have been changed to protect the innocent, the guilty, and anyone in between who might not be comfortable with my dredging up our shared past just so that you can have something fun to read at the beach. Of course, I think that's an exceptionally worthwhile cause that anyone would be proud to embrace, but I don't think the ex-boyfriend I describe as freakishly short or the married guy who hit on me at a singles event would necessarily agree with me.

Thanks so much for buying my book. And to those of you who are reading it in the bookstore because you're undecided or just don't have the cash, I hope that maybe I'll inspire you to whip out your charge card.

Okay, go. Read. Enjoy.

Valentine's Day, Revised

In a perfect world, a woman would never have any charges on her American Express card for Valentine's Day. She'd be treated to dinners at candlelit restaurants and presented with long-stemmed roses and boxes of Belgian chocolates.

In my less than perfect world, relationships always seem to mysteriously evaporate by 11:59 P.M. on February 13, leaving me to pick up my own tab for dinners with friends:

02/14/92	IL VAGABONDO	FOOD/BEVERAGE	33.25
02/14/95	TIVOLI	FOOD AND BEVERAGE	11.00
02/14/99	BOXER'S	FOOD AND BEVERAGE	21.55

I'm embarrassed to say that one year, I stooped to the lowest of lows and sent myself a Valentine's floral arrangement:

02/14/96	800 FLOWERS INC	43.88

The plan was that when my most recent ex stopped by to pick up a jacket I'd borrowed, he'd be overcome with jealousy and would beg me to get back together. As it turned out, the guy didn't come over until the twentieth, by which time I'd been overwhelmed by the stench of mold-covered rose stems and had thrown the whole thing away.

Living in a huge apartment building only makes the holiday more intolerable. Each Valentine's Day, I come home to find the lobby's front desk completely covered with lavish floral arrangements awaiting delivery, and I purposely stroll by in slow motion, hoping the doorman will say, "Oh, Miss Borkowsky, you had some flowers delivered," or even, "A gentleman stopped by earlier and dropped off some chocolates." Instead, Gerard never has to say anything. Except for one year when, noticing my leisurely gait, he remarked, "Good evening, Ms. Borkowsky, did you hurt your foot?"

I wish Valentine's Day were more like Halloween, and single women could knock at the doors of guys we like and collect candy. We'd have a lot more control over things that way, instead of just passively waiting and hoping. We could dress up, not necessarily in costume but in whatever we felt prettiest.

"Who's there?" the guy would ask when we rang the buzzer. "Kiss or treat!" we'd yell. He'd open the door, toss a couple of half-pound boxes of Godiva into our Kate Spade totes, and we'd be on our way.

Club Med Man

On the July Fourth weekend of 1992, at least one American was taking full advantage of her independence and was going off on vacation totally solo.

06/29/92	LIBERTY TRAVEL	TRAVEL PACKAGE	335.00
06/30/92	LIBERTY TRAVEL	TRAVEL PACKAGE	39.00
06/30/92	CLUB MED INC	TKT# 0000000010194	420.00

"What are you running off to Club Med for?" my mother whined into the phone when I explained why I'd be unavailable to attend the once-a-decade cousins' club picnic. "I heard that Club Med is nothing but a bunch of screaming banshees looking to get *shtupped.*"

"It's supposed to be really pretty there," I told her. "It's in Cancún."

"Where is Cancún?" she asked, her tone implying that Cancún must be on the outskirts of Jupiter or Saturn.

"It's in Mexico," I answered, annoyed. I didn't mind giving her a geography lesson, but I felt like I was asking her to sign a consent form for a kindergarten field trip.

"Mexico?" she repeated. "Did I hear you right? You're not going to Mexico, are you?"

"Yes," I said. "I shouldn't have told you. You always find something negative."

I braced myself for the don't-drink-the-water speech I knew was about to come. But she skipped over the water and went directly to the booze: "Y'know Selma Miller said that when her daughter Claudia was there, she went to a bar in what looked like a very nice hotel, and laying in the bottle they poured her drink from was a dead worm."

"Mom, it's supposed to be that way. That's how they do tequila."

"Who sticks a worm inside a drink bottle?" she asked, rhetorically. "I never heard of such a thing."

I vowed that I would not let my mother rain on my Club Med vacation, my bold adventure. As a total non–beach person from Manhattan, I was determined to step beyond my comfort zone and spend a full week in the land of white sand and turquoise waters.

I'd heard that the Club Med environment could be very social, which was part of the reason I'd decided to go there in the first place. But I had never expected the scene I encountered during my first appearance at their tropical open-air bar. I had arrived, it seemed, just in time to catch The Parade of Overly Friendly Men.

"Hi, I'm Jeff from L.A." the blond-and-bland choirboy type said, shaking my hand just a little too warmly.

"Hi, I'm Phil from Portland," another clean-cut guy announced, revealing a blindingly white smile.

"I'm Steve from San Francisco," said the nerdy short guy, planting himself on the barstool beside me.

Just as I was tempted to feel like the It Girl of Cancún, I looked around and realized I was one of barely a dozen women amidst a virtual sea of happy, horny men, there to claim the vacation fling that was their birthright.

After meeting Chip from Irvine, Jason from Seattle, and Matt from San Diego, I was beginning to seriously question whether there was anyone at the club who lived within dating distance of New York, when a tall man with a slightly round face and a New York Yankees cap flashed me a shy smile. "Hey, I'm Marc," he said.

"So, which part of California are you from?" I asked, certain that he wouldn't catch my sarcasm.

"I'm actually from Manhattan," he replied with a laugh, "but I know what you mean. California must be a ghost town now since the entire state is here."

As he stepped back a few paces to place his half-finished Heineken on the bar, I saw that he had at least fifteen extra pounds around his middle, though I had to admire his valiant attempt to camouflage them with a loose-fitting linen shirt. Just a few years earlier, I would have rejected him for the mere crime of possessing a little extra poundage. Now that a string of bad dates had left me stuck and deflated, I was open to the idea that maybe a spare tire was exactly what I needed. After all, I'd read in magazines and heard from married friends that that's the way it works. They say

that when you're *really* ready for a relationship you quit looking for the Mr. Hots and the Mr. Cools and start focusing on
the Mr. Warms—the real, decent, regular guys, which is just
what Marc appeared to be.

I learned he was a financial analyst, and though I had
only a vague notion of what a financial analyst did, I took
the fact that he spelled his name with a "c" as a promising in-
dicator that there might be a bit more offbeatness to him
than met the eye.

"Want to take a stroll along the beach?" he suggested.

"Maybe when the sun goes down," I said. "I burn pretty
easily."

"Okay, can I get you another mai tai?" he offered, as if
the fact that I couldn't take the sun was insignificant. I was
tremendously relieved, since my intense aversion to sun-
bathing had previously resulted in my getting severely
burned over ninety percent of my heart, by more than one
beach-addicted boyfriend.

For the rest of the week, Marc and I were a Couple. We
walked on the beach, talked on the beach, did every clichéd
romantic thing under the sun (after the sun had gone down).
We dined on fine French food at the buffet, and—if you can
count watching Club Med's staff put on skits and hearing
people sing "My Way" at karaoke—we even went to the the-
ater and to concerts.

It was a relief to experience that warm, safe, comfortable
feeling, instead of the nervous excitement I tend to feel
when a guy is too good-looking, too extroverted, or just too
unavailable.

Marc was on the quiet side, but he said the things that mattered. "You're amazing," he whispered on our last night, as I overcame my aversion to idiotic group dances and got up to do the Macarena.

I was starting to think that he was amazing, too, though I wasn't about to do anything stupid, like tell him.

Club Med wasn't just a vacation. It was a honeymoon, with one critical difference: I had stuck to my policy of not getting Fully Involved until I knew for sure that Our Thing would continue once we got back to reality. But my caution proved completely unwarranted when, just ten hours after I'd returned to New York, my phone rang.

"Hey, it's me," Marc said.

"Hi," I said, hoping he couldn't hear the intense relief I felt. He had spared me the time-consuming, emotionally draining task of calling everyone I knew to ask whether they thought The Guy from Club Med would call.

"I just wanted to make sure you got back okay and to see if you were up for getting together next weekend," he suggested.

We made a plan for Saturday, and, as a risk-conscious woman of the nineties, I wasted no time purchasing the very necessary precautionary items for our date:

07/07/92 VICTORIA'S SECRET   LINGERIE   89.12

I was never one to take foolish chances, like being caught without appropriate lingerie. My particular selection was a lacy-but-not-frilly pale pink camisole with matching panties that fit well within my parameters for The First Time garment: something neither too little-girlish nor too slutty, something simple enough that it was conceivable you might have worn it even if you were just going to have dinner with a friend and then home to watch Leno. Then there was the backup selection, the can't-go-wrong simplicity of the black silk bra with corresponding bikini bottom. The impression to avoid was premeditation, which could totally kill the mood of spontaneous seduction. To me, wearing something bright red with shimmery sequins would be as tacky as if a guy arrived at my door in an outfit that reflected way too much optimism: "Hi, Jeff. Love your Ralph Lauren shirt and—is that a Trojan you're wearing, or a knock-off?"

With Saturday feeling like a lifetime away, I was having a hard time not seeing Marc every day, and found myself missing him. Luckily the feeling was mutual, because that Wednesday he called the minute I walked in from work. Apparently, he had been going through intense withdrawal, too.

"Can I come over tonight?" he asked.

Tonight? I look like a chimpanzee tonight, I thought, realizing I had let my hair dry in its naturally fuzzy state rather than giving it the benefit of a smoothing blow-dry.

"It'd be good to see you," I stalled, "but let me just check my book and make sure I'm not forgetting anything. I think I was maybe supposed to grab a late drink with my friend Sara."

Flipping the pages of an Ikea furniture catalog, the ideal checking-my-datebook sound effect, I threw a studied glance in the mirrored closet door. Hair: frizzy but passable if I pulled it back with a barrette. Stomach: slightly bloated but suck-in-able. Legs: nothing a Daisy touch-up couldn't fix.

"Actually, tonight looks fine," I said.

"Okay, so how about if I get there in about forty-five minutes? I really want to see you."

"Can you make it an hour?" I negotiated, leaving barely enough time to run to the drugstore in case I couldn't find a still-useable Daisy.

Fifty minutes later, my enthusiastically early New Boyfriend was standing at my door, looking dapper as ever and appearing much slimmer in his civilian clothes than he had in his swim trunks.

"Come on, let's get comfortable," he said, assertively leading me by the hand to my own couch. "There's something I have to tell you," he added, with an air of Big News, of pomp and circumstance befitting an important proclamation.

"Okay, what?" I asked.

"I think I'm in love," he said.

"Oh, wow, that's—that's so nice," I said, caught off guard. It had been so long since anyone had said that to me without first putting me through at least six months of torture, that I was truly stunned. *But maybe this is the way it's supposed to be when you find The Right One*, I thought. No torture, no head games, just letting it happen.

"I'm in love," he said again, this time more slowly, *"with Shirley."*

"Shirley? Who the hell is Shirley?" I asked, having never before heard the name attached to anyone who wasn't an aunt or married to someone named Seymour.

"I went out with Shirley for two years until last February, and being with you made me realize that I'm still in love with Shirley."

I was shocked. Completely and utterly flabbergasted. This announcement totally violated the unwritten law that clearly states there's an inverse relationship between attractiveness and sweetness. Marc was pudgy and merely pleasant-looking. Pudgy and pleasant-looking guys weren't supposed to dump me. That's what *GQ* guys and JFK Jr. look-alikes were for. Pudgy guys were supposed to be honorable, caring, and sweet.

"I love everything about Shirley," he went on. "My family loved her and all my friends loved her and she has this really adorable laugh, like a little girl really, and she's brilliant and—"

"Why did you even bother coming over?" I interrupted. "You could've just told me this over the phone. It's not like we were dating or anything," I said, trying to minimize things as much to ease my own suffering as to bruise his ego, to let him know that he hadn't really meant that much to me.

"I don't know, I just thought I should tell you in person," he said. "And I wanted to thank you for helping me realize what I really want. If I hadn't met you, I don't know if I would've realized how much I really want to be with Shirley."

I was dying to know what exactly it was about me that had sent him running back to Shirley, but I'd had enough abuse for one night.

"That's okay," I said, still trying to act like he didn't matter. "That's the way these vacation things go. And as long as we're being honest, you weren't my usual type anyway."

07/17/92 VICTORIA'S SECRET   LINGERIE -89.12 (CREDIT)

Celebrity Vision

The night that I joined my friends Sara and Ellie for dinner in one of the Upper West Side's most happening restaurants . . .

09/30/94 CAFE LUXEMBOURG	FOOD/BEV	87.00

. . . it had been approximately six months since I'd bought my six-month supply of disposable contact lenses.

03/14/94 BIMC NY HEALTHCARE	MEDICAL SERVICES	90.00

Not only had I just run out of contacts, but I couldn't find my glasses, either.

Now, in many New York restaurants, this would be a blessing. As someone who's always the first to notice the most minuscule cockroach running around the table, without my contacts I could delude myself into thinking it was merely a hyperactive Milk Dud. But this was Café Luxembourg, known not for bugs but for celebrities, and it would figure that on this night of visual impairment, everyone I could possibly want to see would be there.

"Look, by the window—there's Cyndi Lauper!" Sara said. "She looks great!"

"She hasn't aged a bit," Ellie said.

"She looks like a fuzzy blob," I said.

Two forkfuls of angel-hair pasta later, Sara issued another Celebrity Alert: "Over by the wall. It's Randy Quaid!"

I remembered him being more of a character actor than a hunk, but on this night, I couldn't quite tell.

"He looks fabulous!" Sara said.

"He looks amazing!" Ellie said.

"He looks like a fuzzy blob," I said, squinting, which I'm sure was a huge turn-on for Randy.

Thankfully, Sara had the good judgment to finish chewing her penne primavera before her jaw really dropped: "Over in the corner! It's Nicole Kidman and *Tom Cruise!*"

I couldn't believe it. If there was one celebrity I actually would be excited to see, it was Tom Cruise. And there I was, just twenty feet away from *Tom Cruise's Fuzzy Blob!*

"Ellie, let me borrow your glasses," I said, and my self-sacrificing nearsighted friend allowed me to borrow her very retro black horn-rims, which on me looked exactly like those Halloween glasses with the plastic nose. But I didn't care that I looked ready to trick-or-treat at any moment. I walked straight over to Tom, who was cozied in a rear booth with the lovely, raven-haired Nicole Kidman. I reminded myself to play it cool, really cool, since the last thing I wanted to be was some typical, giddy, gushing fan. I opened my mouth: "I'm sorry for interrupting your dinner but I just had to come say 'hello' because my friends keep seeing all these celebrities and of course tonight was the one time I went out without my contact lenses so I haven't really gotten to see them even though they tell me Cyndi Lauper and Randy Quaid are here and they're great and everything but when they told me Tom Cruise was here I just had to ask my friend Ellie to lend me her glasses so if these glasses look like they're not really right for my face that's 'cause they're not mine and anyway I just wanted to say hello."

"Okay," he said, flashing his perfect white smile. "Thanks for saying hello."

The Dangers of Dating
an Audiophile

Since most of the guys I'd dated had been unusually domesticated creatures, more inclined to fix dinner than stereos, I found it a refreshing change when I met Ed, a video editor, whose comfort fiddling with video equipment extended to a self-proclaimed proficiency at repairing audio systems, light fixtures, kitchen appliances, telephones, answering machines, computers, televisions, electric toothbrushes, washing machines, and hearing aids. He seemed to live his life by the credo "If it ain't broke, if it is broke, or if there's even a small chance it could break at any point in the foreseeable future, fix it."

If he were a doctor, I'm sure he'd get sued for performing unnecessary surgeries. "I'm sorry, doctor," the patient would say, "but I got two other opinions who said they didn't think I needed a hysterectomy."

"It's too bad you feel that way, Mr. Silverman," he'd reply.

Luckily, since Ed was only a boyfriend, he was limited to less life-threatening procedures, like performing a battery transplant on my alarm clock, or doing a dirt-ectomy on my Dustbuster. And when it came to stereo stuff, it was clear he considered matching red plugs to red holes and yellow plugs to yellow holes to be as exciting a hookup as any.

One lazy Sunday morning, three months into our dating bliss, we were lounging around and perusing the Sunday paper when I uttered seven simple words that apparently were the keys to a floodgate: "I'm thinking of buying a new stereo."

His response was immediate. "You're gonna want the cassette player and the CD changer, since you probably still have cassettes you'll want to listen to, but I would stick with just the three-disc changer because the more discs you hold on a multidisc changer the more complex the rotating mechanism becomes and since it takes more power to rotate a bunch of discs versus just three or say five discs max, it places more strain on the motor and then makes the whole thing more likely to malfunction, and besides, the sound quality isn't at all determined by how many CDs the equipment can hold, since it's really the speakers that spit out the sound, and if you're gonna pay a little more, better to invest in decent speakers than to get one of those hundred-disc changers, which didn't get great reviews from *Consumer Reports* anyway, though I can check the ratings again, but I would definitely get the bookshelf speakers I already told you about, which got killer reviews for their price range, and for the output you're getting they're pretty compact, though you really sacrifice nothing on the woofer and the tweeter."

Half zoning out, more from lack of interest than lack of understanding, I nodded approvingly after each sentence. If I ever totally fell for Ed, I realized, I'd have to be comfortable with the idea of becoming an audiophile-phile—someone who's in love with someone who's in love with stereo equipment. At the moment, while not completely fallen, I was quickly losing my balance, sucked in by the warmth and gritty Brooklyn charm packed into his compact but well-muscled body. He had the chocolate-brown eyes and matching hair I always go for, though he was a guy more driven by instinct than intellect, a refreshing change for me.

"Get dressed so we can go," he suggested.

"Go where?"

"I wanna bring you to my guy Maxwell over at Newmark & Lewis—he'll take care of you," he said, with all the importance of a primary-care physician referring me to a top-notch dermatologist.

I've noticed that a man always loves to have His Guy at any establishment, that one employee astute enough to recognize that the company's future will be determined solely by keeping this particular man happy. His Guy makes him feel special, honored, and in the loop. His Guy's last name is usually MyMan.

"Maxwell MyMan, I want you to meet my girlfriend, Amy," Ed said, gesturing toward me as if I were a deluxe washer-dryer combo on a game show. "I'm thinking maybe you could set her up with a receiver and a CD player."

Maxwell MyMan, of course, heard this as, "I'm thinking maybe you could set yourself up with an extra ninety bucks in commission," and responded instantly with a sure-what-did-you-have-in-mind-I'm-happy-to-help-you-guys-out.

Ed glowed with pride, as if he'd merely snapped his fingers and his sound-system soldier had stood at attention.

Now, I was never one to care much about having the latest and greatest stereo equipment. I still can't notice an appreciable difference between the sound of a cassette and a CD, and the system I was replacing was a no-name turntable/cassette/AM-FM unit from my college days that was starting to chew up and spit out my tapes. Which meant that anything, short of a wind-up Victrola, would be a step up. In a blind test, I'd probably find the cheapest CD player just as palatable as the most expensive alternative—but was too embarrassed to say so. On the other hand, I was too savvy a consumer to get suckered into buying a high-end stereo, when a CrapaPhonic All-in-One system would do just fine.

So I was feeling some pressure when Maxwell MyMan made his recommendation: "I could set you up with a top-of-the-line Denon receiver and five-disc changer, a Pioneer deck, and some absolutely phenomenal Bang & Olufsen speakers. All together that'd come to thirty-one hundred dollars—but, well, between you and me, since Ed is such a good customer and I wanna keep you guys happy, I can round it down to an even three grand."

Ed, understandably, had turned on his emotional high beams and was glowing with pride. He'd not only provided me with personalized attention from one of Newmark & Lewis's top salesmen, he'd saved me a hundred dollars to boot.

Having no intention of spending anywhere near three thousand dollars, I nevertheless replied immediately in clear, no-nonsense terms, "Okay, but my building only accepts deliveries Monday through Friday, and make sure the truck gets there by five."

I knew that most retailers of big-ticket items have a cancellation window of at least forty-eight hours, meaning there's an excellent chance you can get out of the whole deal. So I said yes, allowing Ed to save face in front of Mr. MyMan. Everybody was happy for the moment, and I figured that when I canceled the order in a day or two, Ed's ego crash would be a milder, less painful experience.

Or so went the theory.

The next day, hoping to further cushion the blow, I considered serving Ed an Ego Deflation Sandwich: "Honey, I have to say, you totally saved my life with that new power cord for my vacuum. Oh, and by the way, when I called Maxwell this morning 'cause I decided to cancel the receiver and the CD changer, it sounded like he was right next door on the nine-hundred-megahertz phone you recommended."

The sandwich, I knew, would not agree with him, since it was already making me ill. So I opted instead for my usual gentle-but-direct approach. I called Ed from work to break the news. "Thanks for taking me stereo shopping yesterday," I began, "but I woke up in a panic and realized it was way more than I need, so I just called Maxwell to cancel."

"You canceled *all* the stuff?" he asked, sounding totally shell-shocked.

"Yeah, I just had him credit it back to my Amex."

01/20/91 NEWMARK & LEWIS

AUDIO/VIDEO, APPLIANCES —3,212.10 (CREDIT)

"You mean after I spent half a day with you at Newmark &
Lewis and hooked you up with My Guy, you just backed out
of the *whole* thing? Are you fuckin' kidding me?"

"It's not that the stuff wasn't good," I explained. "It was
too good, and it'd be a waste if I wouldn't appreciate it."

"Look, from now on, you're on your own," he threatened.
"There's no point in giving you advice if you're not going to
take it."

Sounds more like an order than advice, I thought. Confused but
feeling bad for Ed, I said nothing.

Stereos. Men. I doubted I'd ever totally understand how
either was wired.

Let There Be Darkness

Any shrink will tell you that waking early is a sign of anxiety.

Any decorator will tell you that waking early is a sign of a crappy window shade.

My bedroom window looks directly out onto the East River, giving me the double whammy of the sunrise *and* its reflection, starting at around seven-thirty in the winter and six-fifteen in the summer. For the entire first year that I lived in my apartment, I would go to sleep in a bedroom and wake up in an interrogation room, the light so blindingly bright that it managed to sneak around the sides of my so-called blackout shade.

Now, if they're going to call it a blackout shade, I expect total darkness. I can't sleep without it, and I've always been a person who needs eight hours. Consequently, I'd often find myself ending dates early. "No, really, I *do* want to get dessert," I'd say, "but I have to go home and get to sleep."

"Why? Do you have a morning meeting tomorrow?"

"No," I'd say. "I have a crappy window shade."

There were some days when I'd doze off at my desk at the ad agency, burnt out from endless nights of sleep deprivation. Unless I was mistaken, it was farmers who were supposed to rise with the sun, not copywriters.

In all fairness to the company that made my first blackout shade, a custom model that I paid good money for . . .

09/30/90 GOLDEN HOME   WINDOW ACCESSORIES   389.17

. . . I'm sure the shade itself was a quality item. Most likely, the problem was simply that the shade was a little too narrow to fully cover my window.

I'd had it for half a year before I finally got around to calling the shade company to come fix it. That then meant, of course, that I'd have to let a strange workman into my bedroom so he could measure my window.

The strange workman plays a very special role in my life, as he is the only man who could potentially end up in my bedroom before we've even had a first date. Thus, having a strange workman over generally requires some preparation:

1. Hide anything of a sexual nature, including but not limited to condoms, diaphragms, vibrators, or zucchinis.

2. Hide anything of value, with the following exceptions: wall unit, sofa, easy chair, or any other item that can't be easily slipped into a toolbox.

3. Close the bathroom door and leave the water running. If the workman looks skeevy, you can yell to your imaginary showering husband: "Honey, the shade man is here!"

Then there's my mother's advice: "Don't wear anything

skimpy that'll give him ideas. Just to be safe, when he rings your buzzer, throw on your down jacket with the hood, and tell him you just got back from a ski trip."

I realized all the concern was for naught when the same clean-cut guy who had installed the shade originally appeared at my door. In a bright white dress shirt and khakis, Isaac looked well-pressed and professional—nothing for me to worry about.

I told him how exhausted I'd been from waking up with the sun, how my work life and even my social life had been totally thrown off by the fireball that shone into my bedroom every morning.

"The problem is your window," he said.

"My window?" I asked. "What's wrong with it?"

"It's crooked."

"It is?" I replied, incredulous that he had the balls to blame the victim.

"Yup, your window is crooked, and that's why you're getting leaking light," he said.

"Look, Isaac," I began, "let's say I give you the benefit of the doubt that, yeah, maybe there is a little symmetry problem with my window, and the light is leaking, okay. You came, you saw, you measured; if, in fact, my window is crooked, and I bought a shade custom-made to fit my window, then shouldn't you have made me a crooked shade?"

"We don't make an uneven shade," he said, with an excess of pride. "We give you a nice, even shade. A lopsided shade would be schlocky, and my boss would *never* let me sell you schlock."

Drawing a deep breath, I promised myself that I would *not* be a sucker for quality. I would hold my ground and stand up for my *right* to an inferior product.

I glared at Isaac and threatened: "If you don't give me a lopsided, schlocky shade by this Friday I'm reporting you to the Better Business Bureau."

"Hey, why's your window shade sitting on the floor?" Ed asked.

"Oh, I have to call and make an appointment for the guy to come back and install it," I explained. "It's the replacement shade they finally sent me, since they took back the one with the light leak."

"They're not gonna charge you to put it up, are they?" he asked.

"Yeah. It's fifty dollars, but they didn't charge me for the shade."

"That's ridiculous," he said. "I can do it for you for nothing."

"I don't know," I hesitated. "Aren't there some special tools you need?"

"Nope, trust me, I must've put in twenty window shades."

"Well, okay," I agreed, eager to see whether or not the new shade would eliminate the dreaded leaking light.

Moments later, Ed was frantically removing every item from the floor of my linen closet. My curling iron, my regular iron, blow-dryer, hammer, screwdriver, all my high school yearbooks, my college yearbook, and various boxes of nails and tacks, all placed in my bathroom hallway.

"Are we having a rummage sale?" I asked.

"No," Ed said, completely unoffended by my sarcasm, one of his endearing qualities. "I was just looking for your carbide chuck drill."

"What's a carbide chuck drill?" I asked.

"It has a lock to hold the bits in," he said. "I can't believe you don't have a carbide chuck drill. We'd better go pick one up."

"Are they expensive?"

"Nah," he assured me. "We can probably go over to Twenty-third Street and get our hands on a used one for twenty or thirty bucks, tops. I'll call My Guy over at the electric supply place and see what he can do."

04/04/90 KIPS BAY	HARDWARE	118.89

After making what Ed had convinced me was an investment in a brand-new drill, I settled into my couch to watch a murder trial on Court TV until, nearly two hours later, I heard Ed calling out frantically, "Honeyyyyyyyyyy, come look! The shade is lopsided!"

"I know!" I yelled back, not wanting to miss the verdict in the case of a crazed socialite accused of brutally murdering her doctor husband. "I had them make it that way 'cause the window's lopsided!"

"Well, then, they put the lop on the wrong side!" he yelled back, and even after a commercial break had freed me to join him in the bedroom, he was still yelling: "Look! The left side is overlapping on the window frame while there's a huge gap on the right side!"

Taking the volume down a few notches, I said, in a very matter-of-fact tone, trying my best not to sound accusatory, "You hung it backwards. The shade should roll down from over the top, not be pulled from underneath."

"Are you sure?" he asked, incredulous.

"Yeah," I said. "The rope pull is supposed to be attached on the window side, where you don't see the tack."

"Holy shit, you're right," he noted, clearly stunned and, I suspect, wounded.

Dipping into my jar of salve for wounded pride, I offered, "They should have a this-side-up sticker, or something, 'cause otherwise the obvious assumption is that it could go either way, like a roll of toilet paper. I don't know how those idiots expect anyone to know which way is which."

"I can't believe it," he said.

"I'm just impressed you even got it up there," I said. "Look, why don't we just leave it for tonight, and I can deal with it tomorrow."

"Let me take one more crack at it," he insisted, "and maybe I can just yank it out and flip it around."

Calculating the potential time and money the yanking-out process might add to the costs for reinstallation, I resolved that there was no way in this universe that I was going to let Ed take another crack.

"It's okay," I said, "I'll just have the installer come out. He'll probably have an electric yanker-outer in his truck."

"Really, it'd be no big deal to redo it," he said, though I could sense his relief.

"Well, if the shade guy can't get it in there, I may take

you up on it," I said, fairly sure such a scenario would not come to pass.

"Sounds like a plan," he agreed. "Anyway, I'm beat. I feel like I'm coming down with something."

04/20/90 GOLDEN HOME   WINDOW ACCESSORIES   50.00

The Scariest Gift

One night, I was working late at the ad agency when I called my home machine and got a message from Donald Duck: "Hey, how ah ya doin'? It's me," he quacked. I was wondering how Donald got my number, until he said: "Ah'm feeling so lousy, ah had to miss mah edit session."

Unless Donald Duck had developed a sudden interest in video editing, I realized, it must be a congested version of Ed.

I called him back. "You sounded really awful. I almost didn't recognize you."

"I just took my temperature," he said. "It's a hundred and two."

"Do you feel up to company later?" I asked, hoping for a no since I was deep in the midst of work and couldn't afford to get sick.

"Nah," he answered, "I think I just need to sleep it off."

Wanting to comfort him in some way, I racked my brain for what to do. I could send him flowers, but with his allergies they'd only make him more congested. A bouquet of balloons was out, since they'd fill up half his studio, and a Strip-o-Gram would, I feared, only make him hotter.

Finally, inspiration struck, and I picked up the phone.

"Hi, I was wondering—if I gave you guys my charge card number, could you send something over to my boyfriend's apartment?"

04/03/90 THIRD AVE SANDWICH   FOOD/BEV   3.75

For two seventy-five and a dollar tip, I decided to send him some chicken soup—a gift that would not only wish him well but could actually help him get there.

Thirty minutes later, my phone rang again. "Oh my God," Ed said. "I can't believe you did that."

Not quite sure whether he was going to thank me for the soup or bawl me out for something else, I asked for clarification. "You can't believe I did what?"

"Sending over that soup was the *most unbelievable thing* anyone's *ever* done for me," he said, in a tone that was a bizarre blend of appreciation and—I knew I wasn't imagining it— sheer terror.

Had I been *too* nice? Was I showing that I cared too much, letting on that I was actually into him?

"I just figured it'd be something a little different than a get-well card," I said, in a feeble attempt to diffuse the impact of what I had not realized was such a Grand Gesture.

"I'm stunned," he said, followed by an appropriate stunned silence. "This was just so *unbelievably nice*."

The Beach Versus Me

While I love to vacation *on* the water,

03/30/94	CUNARD LINE LTD	CRUISE	603.00
03/22/95	CARNIVAL CRUISE RESERVATION		879.50

and can think of nothing more soothing than dining with a water view,

07/22/88	RACHEL'S RESTAURANT	OCEAN BEACH	14.50
07/24/88	WALLY'S PLACE	OCEAN BEACH	20.95

I am terrified of actually going *in* the water. I am also not at all comfortable baring my cellulite to strangers, which can lead to only one conclusion: I am not a beach person.

If my lover and I were running toward each other on a beach in slow motion, I would keep right on running if I knew that just past him was an air-conditioned Barnes & Noble.

So it figures that just about every guy I've ever really been excited about has been a beach person.

One night, Ed and I were at a Japanese restaurant, sitting

on a tatami mat and making fairly idle chitchat when he said, with a slight tremble in his voice, "Amy, there's something I've been wanting to ask you."

With totally feigned coolness, I replied, "Ask away," though from the corner of my eye I glanced at his plate, looking for the ring hidden in his tuna sashimi.

"I was wondering if you'd," he began, and then he began again: "I just wanted to know if you, if you, y'know, if you, if you *like the beach*."

He looked up hopefully, as if he'd just asked me to donate a kidney and desperately needed to know if I'd be a match.

"Well, actually," I began, the two words an attempt to buy some time, to come up with a more delicate phrasing than what actually slipped out, "I hate the beach."

From the pained expression on his face, I knew immediately what I'd done.

I had put a chopstick through his heart.

After a long and unsettling pause, he probed, "But you do go to the beach *sometimes*, right? Like in the summer, you do go and lay out, right, just kind of bake in the sun a little and chill?"

"No," I answered, "I don't bake."

"So you're not a beach person, then, huh?" he asked, giving me one last chance to save the relationship, to save the lives of our future children.

And with visions of a thousand more nerdy singles events dancing in my head, I did my best to backpedal. "Well, I wouldn't go that far," I said. "'Not a beach person' is a pretty strong statement. I mean, I do go to the beach *occasionally*."

"But when was the last time you actually went swimming in the ocean?" he asked.

"When I went with my friend Lori's family to L.A., we had a great time swimming at Hermosa Beach."

"When was that?"

"Nineteen seventy-nine."

"So you haven't been to a beach in *eleven years*?"

"No, no, I've been *to* the beach," I desperately explained. "I just haven't been lying in the sun or swimming in the ocean. But I *love* the sound the waves make when they crash against the shore, and, well, for the longest time I've been meaning to buy one of those sleep-machine things that plays the sound of waves 'cause it's just *so* relaxing, and—"

Cutting through my b.s., he said, "Yeah, but you're saying you don't ever lay out, go swimming, that kind of thing, right?"

"And I *love* looking out the window of my apartment and watching the sailboats go by," I continued and realized I was backpedaling up a very steep hill.

"Those aren't sailboats," he corrected me. "They're garbage barges."

"Well, whatever. You get my point."

"Yeah," he concluded. "It sounds like this isn't going to work, because I'm a total beach person."

I'm sorry to say that after that night, Ed and I went directly into Breakup Mode, seeing each other just long enough to get a couple of CDs, a few T-shirts, and one carbide chuck drill back to their rightful owners. I'll always believe it was the chicken soup that did it, that made him realize he could have something real with me if he wanted it, a thought that must've been scary enough to make him run. But a girlfriend of mine saw him at party not long ago and said that, when my name came up he said it was a shame that it hadn't worked out but that he just couldn't see himself ending up with someone who didn't love the beach. So maybe that *was* it, after all.

Still, it's sad to think that two people in the same zip code could be separated by an ocean.

A Big-Enough Bed

In case I somehow didn't get the message that I was totally alone on this particular Valentine's Day, Jensen-Lewis, a trendy New York furniture store, chose February 14 to put through the charge for the final payment on my new queen-sized bed, the first bed I had ever owned that was truly roomy enough for two.

02/14/91 JENSEN-LEWIS	760.00

I had given a lot of thought to what size bed I wanted. I figured the queen reflected optimism that I wouldn't spend my life as a nun (a prediction in which I felt especially confident, since I'm Jewish). On the other hand, the king reflected an optimism so extreme, it could end up jinxing me.

More Queen Latifah than Queen Elizabeth, the bed I chose was a funky matte-black wooden platform style, with a small nightstand attached on either side. It was called the Ice House Bed because the headboard consisted of a row of glass blocks that looked a lot like jumbo ice cubes. With the flick of a button, I could make the whole row glow with a soft, clear light.

I moved recently, and since I decided to do my new bed-room in a zenlike style with subdued light woods, I put my funky black bed up for sale on craigslist.com. Within a day I managed to sell it to a good-looking Wall Street guy named Chip.

It figures. There'll finally be a man sleeping in my bed next Valentine's Day, and I won't be there to enjoy it.

Amy the Amazing Hula Hooper

Back when I was in fifth grade and it was time to pick teams for softball or soccer, I'll admit, quite humbly, that I was the kid everyone fought over.

"You take her!" one team captain would scream.

"No, *you* take her!" the other captain would yell back. "We got stuck with her last time!"

A total spazz in all traditional athletic exploits, I was nevertheless an idiot savant when it came to hula hooping.

For reasons I still can't begin to fathom, I had the un-canny ability to keep that hot-pink plastic ring circling around my emaciated waist for minutes on end, whirling round and round until, one by one, the neighborhood kids who'd gathered would wander away (at which point I'd let the hoop drop to the ground, because if a hula hoop stays up in a forest and nobody sees it, what's the point, right?).

It's not surprising, then, that I turned to the hula hoop years later as a response to my mother's frantic message about the importance of regular exercise, which she'd read in an article on blood clots in *Redbook* or *Good Housekeeping* or one of her other scholarly journals.

Normally not one to act on my mother's often sketchy information, half of which I suspect she embellishes to meet her own agendas, I thought that this general advice, trying to get more exercise, was sound. But I spent most of my days and nights sitting at a desk, and my only connection to any gym was that I had once entered a place called the Vertical Club on Fifty-ninth Street to use the ladies' room. The hula hoop seemed, to me, a much more convenient and enjoyable option.

05/11/91 TOYS "R" US	TOYS	3.87

When I got the hoop home and took it for a spin, I was thrilled to see that, even after so many years, I still had it. I raised the hoop to my waist, gave it one good push, and was able to hoop my way through an entire *Unsolved Mysteries* segment, about two girls who grew up in an orphanage in England and fifty years later found each other in a Burger King in Cleveland.

Hula hooping was but one of the many activities I took up when, after realizing I was fairly settled in my advertising career, I decided to embrace the mantra Be All You Can Be:

09/12/91 FRENCH INSTITUTE	TUITION/FEES/BOOKS	155.00
10/28/91 THE LEARNING ANNEX	SEMINARS	30.50
01/04/92 THE LEARNING ANNEX	SEMINARS	25.00
03/12/92 PARLIAMO ITALIANO	TUITION/FEES/BOOKS	195.00

I took French lessons, film classes, acting classes. I became
The Overscheduled Adult, determined to acquire that *je ne
sais quoi*, or at least to learn a method for faking it.

I bought storage cubes to organize my life,

02/02/92 LECHTERS	HOUSEWARES/ACCESSORIES	46.19

and videos on how to do anything and everything better.

04/25/92 HOW TO VIDEO SOURCE	VIDEO SALES/RENTAL	41.02
04/28/92 HOW TO VIDEO SOURCE	VIDEO SALES/RENTAL	20.51

I even reupholstered my chairs,

03/15/92 DIXIE FOAM LTD	173.20

though the last thing I wanted to do was just sit around.

I had a persistent, gnawing feeling that there was something bigger and better out there for me, a destiny grander
than writing ads for frozen vegetables. So I was thrilled to
see this ad in *Backstage* magazine: "Do you have an unusual
talent? National TV show seeks offbeat, odd, and outrageous acts. Auditions will be held this Saturday at South
Street Seaport's Pier 17, from 2 to 5 pm."

The next morning, as I stood in the bathroom brushing
my teeth, I strained to think of a certifiably outrageous act I
could do. I gazed into the mirror, my brushstrokes becoming
faster and more intense, as if they could stimulate my brain
to come up with something.

I was particularly encouraged by the fact that nowhere in

the ad did it say you had to be *good* at what you did. You just had to be *offbeat, odd,* or *outrageous.*

My thoughts drifted back to my hula hoop, and I wondered if there were any tricks I might be able to pull off. Then I realized that the inspiration I'd been searching for was staring me in the face. Literally.

I could hula hoop *and brush my teeth simultaneously.* I would be Amy the Amazing Toothbrushing Hula Hooper!

I would be the first woman on Earth to swivel her hips *and prevent tooth decay* at the same time!

Four out of five dentists surveyed would recommend me to their patients who watch novelty acts!

I would hang posters all over the city: SHOW BUSINESS NOW CONTAINS FLUORIDE!

But was the whole thing too nuts? I worried. Was I ready to be seen foaming at the mouth on national TV, to risk being billed as both a dental case and a mental case?

Hedging my bets, I realized I needed a backup shtick, something else to combine with the hula hooping in case they thought the toothbrushing stuff was too bizarre or, from a more practical standpoint, just too darn messy. So that Saturday, I found myself at the South Street Seaport with my hula hoop, a snazzy new medium-bristle toothbrush, a tube of toothpaste, and—just in case—a push-button princess-style telephone for my alias, Amy the Amazing Phone-Calling Hula Hooper.

I started with the tamer phone bit, rotating the hoop around my waist while balancing the old desktop phone in my right hand and holding the receiver in my left, whining with an exaggerated Brooklyn accent: "Hullo? Op-a-rayta?

Op-a-rayta? I think I was cut awf! I'm trying to reach five faw faw, faw one faw faw." After an initial burst of tepid applause, I felt like I was losing the audience, and, just one minute into my act, my gut screamed at me to go in for The Big Finish. Still keeping the hoop aloft, I said, "Thank you, Op-a-rayta," slammed down the receiver, let the hoop glide slowly to my ankles, and bowed.

"That was fabulous!" a guy in a white T-shirt yelled as the crowd of thirty or so onlookers again applauded weakly. *Fabulously idiotic*, I thought to myself, feeling more than a bit humiliated.

"I have one more thing I do," I said, hoping to whip the crowd into a frenzied, toothpastey froth.

"Let's see it," White T-shirt Guy said.

Quickly patting my jacket pocket to make sure the tube of Crest was still there, I took my toothbrush out of the Duane Reade shopping bag. I confidently stepped into the hoop, gave it one good push, and begin gyrating. Then, lifting my hand, I waved my toothbrush in the air.

I was hooping, and the crowd—now sixty or seventy strong—was whooping.

With my one free hand, I reached into my jacket pocket and, holding up the Crest for all to see, began swinging it around with all the seductiveness of a stripper waving her just-removed bra.

As I carefullly squeezed a blob of toothpaste onto the brush, the screaming and applause grew stronger.

The tension welled up inside of me as I was about to perform my pièce de résistance: the actual brushing. By this point I had kept my hoop going without dropping it for *over two minutes.* I stuck the brush in my mouth, instantly knowing in every fiber of my being that I was offbeat. I was unique. I was outrageous.

I was also gagging.

My mouth was overflowing with Crest, and I realized *I needed to spit.*

Trying to maintain my composure, I jiggled the toothbrush in the void of my mouth, a cagey move that gave the appearance of actual brushing while not creating additional foam.

I was about to choke, and I did not want to die of minty freshness.

Just then I looked up to see my guardian angel. The guy in the white T-shirt stood before me with a small bowl. "It's to spit in," he said.

I spat. I dropped the hoop, bowed, then stood up with my arms extended skyward for a big "Ta-da!"

After a raucous round of applause and another bow, I had victoriously completed my debut performance as Amy the Amazing Toothbrushing Hula Hooper.

The following day, my friend Adam called. "Yvonne and I were driving to Block Island and they were talking about you on the radio."

"They were?" I asked, incredulous.

"Yeah," he confirmed. "They had one of the producers on from that show you tried out for, and when they asked him if he saw any really unusual acts, he said there was some girl who hula hooped and brushed her teeth at the same time."

Wow, I was Some Girl. I was in the running, on the producer's radar screen, and there was, I thought, a better-than-average chance that I would be selected.

When days went by, and eventually weeks, without a phone call or letter from anyone at the show, it would be an understatement to say that I started to get antsy. *What was the hold-up here?* I wondered. Could they possibly have found an act more offbeat or outrageous than mine? Some wacko chick who juggles chainsaws and shaves her armpits at the same time?

After making a convoluted chain of phone calls, I finally managed to track down someone at Vin DiBona Productions.

"Oh, yeah, I definitely remember you," a chipper female voice said. "You're the one who brushed her teeth and hula hooped. We're still editing, but I'd say there's an excellent chance you'll be in the cut."

The word "chance" meant that if I told everyone I knew that I might be on and then I wasn't, I'd feel like a total idiot.

And then the realization hit me: the word "chance" also meant that I *could* be on, and when my family, friends, ad cronies, and former dates all saw me shaking my hips and spewing Crest, I could potentially feel like an even bigger idiot.

In fact, if my dream became a reality, I just might feel like The Biggest Idiot in the World.

I was thrilled. I was petrified. I was conflicted.

Two days later, my phone rang. "Hi, this is Manny Errol calling from Los Angeles," the fast-talking voice on the other end said. "Can I speak with Amy Borkowsky?"

"This is she," I answered, expectantly.

"Like I said, this is Manny Errol," he repeated, as if I was supposed to recognize the name. "I represent novelty acts in Europe and, well, pretty much all over the world. I hear that you do some interesting things with a hula hoop."

"Yeah, I call myself Amy the Amazing Toothbrushing Hula Hooper," I said, amazed that word of my odd, offbeat, and outrageous talent had spread so quickly.

"So, basically, you brush your teeth while you hula hoop?" he clarified.

Hearing a hint of concern that maybe there wasn't quite enough there to play the London Palladium, I added, "Well, it's not just the brushing."

"What else do you do?" He sounded more than a little intrigued.

"I also floss," I said, certain that with an hour's practice I could combine the dual arts of hula hooping and plaque removal for my encore performance, "Amy Unwaxed."

"They'd just love this kind of thing in Germany," Manny said, and I could practically hear him salivating. "It's the kind of thing they go nuts for over in Europe. Your act sounds really visual, so you won't run into a language barrier."

My ambivalence was quickly fading as I realized that I didn't know a soul in Germany, or anywhere else in Europe. This could be the opportunity of a lifetime—a chance to quit my job at the ad agency and hula hoop my way around the world in total anonymity! I could see London, I could see France, and I could *not care* if anyone saw my underpants!

"Do you have a video?" he asked. "I really have to see this."

"Not yet," I said, "but I'll borrow a camera from a friend and make one this weekend."

09/20/92 KIM 44 DISCOUNT	AUDIO/VIDEO	1,080.59
09/22/92 KIM 44 DISCOUNT	AUDIO/VIDEO	-1,080.59
		(CREDIT)

I jotted down Manny's address, hung up the phone, and poured myself a celebratory glass of guava juice. The show hadn't even aired and already Hollywood was calling.

Three weeks later, I was sitting down to a lovely dinner of Ben & Jerry's Chocolate Chip Cookie Dough Lowfat Yogurt when my friend Ellie called.

"Turn on the TV!" she yelled excitedly. "They just said *America's Funniest People* is coming up next! It sounds like the show you tried out for!"

Ben, Jerry, and I plopped ourselves down on the couch just in time to hear the opening music, a quirky little country tune, accompanied by a montage of shots: a fat guy jiggling his belly, an old lady doing a headstand, a girl in a polka-dot blouse with frizzy Jewish hair—wait, that's *my* frizzy Jewish hair, and I'm hula hooping and holding a princess phone, and—wow, they've already cut away to a Chinese woman making a pig face.

Over in a fleeting second, it wasn't even a brush with fame. It was a single bristle, and without a drop of tooth-paste. *What happened to the toothbrushing shot?* I wondered.

The phone rang again. "Was that you?" Ellie asked.

"You couldn't tell?" I replied, a little disappointed but

mostly relieved that the people at work wouldn't recognize me.

"You have to admit," Ellie said, "if you bent down to clip a hangnail, you would've missed your whole thing."

The next morning, I learned that nobody at my office had clipped a hangnail on the previous night between 8:00 and 8:02 P.M.

"You were awesome!!!" screamed Rick, the receptionist.

"Congratulations!" cheered Phillip, the account exec.

"You're famous!" chirped Sue, the strategic planner.

"I saw some nut on TV who looked just like you," said Jim, a creative director.

"How do you know it wasn't me?" I asked.

"This girl was hula hooping with a telephone, and I know you'd never do anything that dopey."

My worst fear was materializing. I was a nut. I was dopey. I was The Biggest Idiot in the World.

Go figure: half a dozen people thought my act was cool, then one guy vomits and it's all I focus on. When would I learn to quit caring so much about what people think and just have fun?

Eventually time passed and my hula hoop dreams faded. I left the job where I was writing ads for frozen broccoli and got a bigger, better job writing commercials for a major bank. I went to important meetings and dressed the part:

03/26/93 BLOOMINGDALE'S		
	LADIES SUITS AND BLAZERS	219.16
03/29/93 ANN TAYLOR	COORDINATES	601.76

I gave up my quest to Be All I Could Be and decided to try to be content in my very nice job that allowed me to Buy All I Could Buy:

04/16/93 MADISON SQUARE GARDEN		
PARAMOUNT CONCERT	255.00
07/20/93 GILES & LEWIS LTD GALLERY	500.00
09/17/93 HOTEL TORNABUONI FIRENZE	
LIRE BILLED AS 458,500	291.66
11/21/93 MACY'S BETTER CONTEMPORARY DRESS	219.09
12/02/93 MACY'S BETTER RELATED SEPARATES	187.88

And then Hollywood came calling again.

Okay, technically the call was from Forty-fifth Street and Broadway in Manhattan. But I'd been cranking out bank ad after bank ad and was losing interest in interest rates, so I found it to be the perfect wake-up call.

"Hi, I'm a producer for *The Jon Stewart Show* at MTV," said the friendly woman on the phone. "I hear you have an act you do with a hula hoop, and I was wondering if you'd be able to come in and audition for us tomorrow at three."

Wow. It'd been over a year since I'd hung up my hula hoop. I owed it to myself to follow through, to see where my old hula hoop dream could take me.

"Tomorrow at three sounds great," I replied, fully aware that I had a meeting with the bank client at two and would be lucky to be finished by four-thirty. I could get out of it, but how would the account executive explain my absence? Then I realized that with all that toothbrushing, I had a great excuse: "I'm not going to make it to the meeting tomorrow," I regretfully informed the account executive. "I have a dental appointment."

That night, I scrambled to MTV-ify my act. Making a mad dash to the toy store, I picked up the hippest hoop I could find, in an electric shade of neon green:

01/11/94 TOYS "R" US	TOYS	4.18

A quick stop at the drugstore and I was amazed to find a choice of *two different models* of neon green toothbrushes. I bought the medium bristle *and* the velvet-touch:

01/11/94 DUANE READE	PRESCRIPTIONS/SUNDRIES	7.19

I ran to the record store and found the perfect musical accompaniment, a song called "Round and Round" by Tevin Campbell:

01/11/94 SAM GOODY	MUSIC/ACCESSORIES	16.21

And being someone who always needs a backup plan, I stayed up thinking of an alternate shtick until four A.M., nearly pulling a muscle in my cranium when I finally hit upon something so highbrow, so utterly intellectual, that even if the MTV folks ended up hating it, there was no way it could make me feel like the biggest idiot in the world. For my Plan B, I would hula hoop while reciting the famous balcony soliloquy from *Romeo and Juliet*. I'd call it "Shakespeare in the Round."

When I arrived for the audition, I was immediately ushered into a large conference room where a bevy of fresh-faced producers sat around a mammoth table, at the head of which was none other than Jon Stewart himself.

Fueled by a burning ambivalence, a crystal-clear sense of doubt, I knew at that moment that hula hooping in public for me was much more than a dream.

It was a nightmare.

Reading the room, I could practically smell the intelligence, and I knew what I had to do.

I clenched an old Samuel French script from my brief stint at acting school, started hooping with abandon, and, in an exaggerated Brooklyn accent, pleaded, "Romeo, Romeo, whehfaw aht thou Romeo?" As I whined out "Deny thy fatha," I began to punctuate each line with a thrust of the hips, transforming myself into a veritable hula hooker. This was my big chance to be on MTV, and I was gonna sex it up! I would be smart *and* sexy, and maybe even dopey, but I was bound and determined to be on MTV.

My moment of doubt had passed, my commitment was palpable, and the producers went nuts, shouting out raves like:

"Do you have a headshot?"

"Could you go for a full minute if you had to?"

"How does your schedule look for next week?"

A flip-flopper no longer, I whipped out my toothbrush and cued up "Round and Round" to cheers of "Does it have to be Tevin Campbell or could you do it to something that's public domain?"

"Could you pull your hair back? It's getting in your face. We'll need to see your face."

"We have your day and night numbers, right?"

I still have the answering-machine message: "Hi, I'm calling from MTV and we'd love to book you to be on Jon's show on February seventeenth."

But it's probably for the best that I don't have a tape from the time the producer called to let me know that, unfortunately, the network was canceling *The Jon Stewart Show*, and they wouldn't be needing me after all.

It's odd that just as I was renewing my commitment, MTV was backing away from theirs. But I'm an optimist, and I'd like to think that maybe, just maybe, Fate stepped in to save me from looking like The Biggest Idiot in the World.

Don't Judge a Book...

My friend Jennifer had been dating her former boss for five years, and I knew that what she really wanted for her birthday was something I couldn't give her: an engagement ring.

I love Jenn, but not quite that much. So the day before her thirtieth-birthday brunch, while browsing at Barnes & Noble, I found what I thought would be the next best thing: a book called *Getting to "I Do."*

The only problem was, as with any self-help book, leaving a title like that hanging around the house could create more issues than it would resolve. Though I hadn't read *Getting to "I Do"* myself, I highly doubted that the author would suggest a strategy that involved your guy finding your copy.

"Why're you reading this?" he'd ask.

"Oh, it's . . . it's . . . it's not mine," you'd stutter. "It's for my sister."

"That's interesting. Didn't your sister just have her twelfth anniversary?"

Then it occurred to me: if clothing companies can make

a reversible jacket, why not the book publishers? Why couldn't the jacket for *How to Get a Man to Propose* have a flip side with a title no guy would be interested in—like *The Big Book of Feelings* or *Shoe Shopping Made Easy!* or *Go with the Flow: Real-Life Adventures in Menstruation?* Since the self-help publishers have yet to be quite so creative, I had to improvise and found an appropriately sized jacket from some how-to book about hair and makeup.

Out of courtesy to Jennifer, I won't reveal the title in case it ever gets back to her boyfriend, who—I say with some pride—is now her husband.

Be My Guest

American Express has what they call Be My Guest gift cer-
tificates, which entitle the recipient to a certain amount of
money toward dinner at any restaurant that accepts Amer-
cian Express. I gave a Be My Guest certificate as a wedding
present to my old high school friend Sandra, and one to our
mutual friend Lori when she got married:

07/06/89 BE MY GUEST SERVICE CHARGE	3.50
12/13/92 BE MY GUEST SERVICE CHARGE	3.50

I think cash is too impersonal a gift and don't buy into the
logic of people who see it as payback for the bride and
groom, who've had to shell out over a hundred dollars a
plate for dinner. What's even less tasteful, I think, is a trend
I've been hearing about on the news where couples recoup
their costs by getting advertisers to sponsor their wedding.
Can you imagine being at the reception and hearing "Now
please clear the dance floor as the bride and groom dance to
their song, the Kit Kat Bar jingle"?

And how would a rabbi work a commercial into a wedding ceremony? "As you perform the centuries-old Jewish tradition of stepping on the glass, should someone get injured, please remember Jacoby and Meyers. Mazel tov.".

I think weddings are just a cost you have to bear. But ask me again when it's me getting married.

New Year's Eve

When you're single in late December and don't have a date for New Year's Eve, you never quite give up hoping that one may materialize. So it was one December 27th when The Tall Guy with the Prematurely Gray Hair—a nameless divorced neighbor I'd spoken to a couple of times in the elevator and had a minor crush on—surprised me as he caught up with me in the lobby and asked: "I know it's last-minute and everything, but I was wondering if you happened to be free for New Year's."

"I may be going to a party," I said, not wanting to appear totally planless, "but I'm not really sure yet."

"When will you know?" he asked. "Because you seem like a nice person, and I figured, hey, why not take a chance and see if you might like to baby-sit."

Baby-sit? I finally get an invitation to New Year's and it's to watch some guy's kids? Does he think that just because I'm female and not wearing a wedding ring I want to spend New Year's Eve changing his kids' stinky diapers and watching the Rugrats Chanukah video?

"I'm not really up for it," I said with a forced smile. "But if you're around on New Year's Day, why don't you stop by? I could use someone to help me carry my old coffee table to the storage room."

The next day, when I'd already happily agreed to go out to dinner with friends on New Year's Eve, I got a call from Jay, the square-jawed psychologist I'd met a few nights earlier, on Christmas Eve, at the Matzoh Ball, New York's annual big bash for Jewish singles. Frankly, I was surprised he had called, since we'd talked for a grand total of fifteen minutes, tops. From what I could tell, he seemed intelligent enough, definitely had a sharp sense of humor, and his jaw gave him an almost chiseled, model-like profile.

"So, what're you doing this weekend?" he asked, as if it were any ordinary weekend and not the one that happened to include New Year's Eve, the most emotionally charged night of the year, next to Valentine's Day.

"I'm going out to dinner with friends on Saturday," I said, just as casually, and added, "If you want to join us, that'd be great."

Just like that, I had asked Jay out for New Year's. We were down to the wire, but I now officially, kind of, had a date for New Year's Eve.

The next night, at the trendy Time Cafe, four of my closest friends, one guy I barely knew, and I all clinked our glasses for a pre–New Year's toast.

It wasn't long before I realized I'd like to get to know Jay better. "I'm all for the warmth and goodwill," Jay said to me, "but I never understood the rationale for knocking the glasses together."

"Me neither," I agreed. "If we were just having food, we wouldn't go banging our plates together, right?"

"Yeah, and it's a really good thing people don't do this when they're snowmobiling," he added, "because if you're each doing fifty miles an hour, the tradition could kill you."

I forgave him for laughing loudly at his own joke, and the rest of the night was filled with more laughter, liquor, and easy conversation. Jay's appetite was as hearty as his laugh, and when the waitress came around for dessert, he ordered the warm flourless chocolate cake, with seemingly no concern about fitting a round dessert into a square jaw.

Then he stood up and excused himself: "Got to pay a visit to the little boys' room."

I admired his bravery for leaving the table—surely he knew that the restroom break is the traditional time for the reviews to come out. And after several minutes of polite chitchat, the critics spoke:

"You guys are cute together," said my friend Adam.

"I agree," said Adam's girlfriend, Yvonne.

"Does he have a brother?" asked Sara.

"Does he have a sister?" asked Danny.

"Does he have the runs?" asked Ellie.

"The runs?" I shuddered. "That's disgusting! What are you talking about?"

"It's been almost fifteen minutes since the guy left to go to the bathroom," Ellie said. "Someone should go check and see what happened to him."

Unbelievably, I had lost track of time in, of all places,

the Time Cafe, where a huge clock graced the wall behind
the bar.

"She's right," I said. "Danny, can you go check in the
men's room and see if he needs help?" Being a veterinarian,
Danny was the only one at the table with any sort of medical
training and so seemed the best choice to rescue Jay, though
I can't imagine Danny had seen many patients who had con-
sumed too much champagne on New Year's. Still, confident
that he could handle whatever might come up—I'd personally seen him perform an emergency spaying on a kitchen
table, and surely Jay's condition wouldn't require measures
that drastic—I continued caking and champagning my way
into the first moments of the new year.

When the coffee arrived, I carefully placed saucers over
Jay's and Danny's cups to keep them warm. I looked at the
clock and now I really was worried. Danny, too, had been
gone for nearly fifteen minutes. Where were they? Was there
a hostage situation in the men's room? Were they victims of
a Mafia hit? Had they been sucked into some big dark restroom vortex, hurled toward some unknown netherworld,
never to be seen again?

"I'll be back in a minute," I said, excusing myself with a
phrase I never thought I'd utter: "I have to go to the men's
room."

I didn't plan to go *into* the men's room—my Missing in
Action companions had already proven that was too risky—
but I could crack the door and call to them from the outside.

I was barely two steps from the table when I saw Danny
heading back, defeated. "He's not in the bathroom," he re-

ported. "I checked the bar downstairs, and he's not at the pay phone, either."

"Let me talk to the coat-check girl," I said, "and see if his jacket's still there."

"Do you remember the guy I came in with, who had the brown leather motorcycle jacket?" I asked.

"You mean the dirty-blondish guy with the square jaw?"

"Yeah, that's him."

"He picked up his jacket a half-hour ago."

Guys had disappeared on me before—suddenly quit calling or, on rare occasions, even stood me up—but this was the first time one had vanished right in the middle of a date. Leaving my friends and me with the tab for a five-course meal, no less:

12/31/94 TIME CAFE	FOOD/BEV	311.76

"Let's call him and see what the hell is going on," Danny insisted. "This is total bullshit."

"I only have his work number," I said.

Danny wrote down the number and vowed to do whatever it took to see justice done.

I don't know what magic Danny worked, but justice came more swiftly than I could possibly have imagined. The next afternoon, Shabbir, the doorman from my building, called me at my office: "Somebody came by today and dropped off an envelope that looks like it has cash in it."

"Was it a guy with dirty blond hair and a square jaw?" I asked.

"Yeah, his hair was dirty blond," he said, "but it was hard to tell the rest because the bottom of his face was covered with a bandage."

Danny still swears that all he did was call the guy, and he's so gentle with animals, I totally believe him.

AUTHOR'S NOTE: If you have any information regarding Jay The Square-Jawed Psychologist and his reason for running out of the Time Cafe in the wee hours of January 1, 1994, please contact Unsolved Dating Mysteries by emailing HiAmila@aol.com.

The Dos and Don'ts of Check Diving

Anyone who's ever witnessed women over sixty settling a restaurant check knows that the I'll-get-it-no-please-I-insist argument can get as fierce as any wrestling match. I fully expect that it's only a matter of time before ESPN catches on and starts bringing us nationally televised Check Diving competitions. Soon, bookies will be taking bets on whether Gloria or Estelle will end up snagging the tab for the Early Bird Specials.

And now, thanks to the American Express Membership Miles program,

09/28/94 MEMBERSHIP MILES	25.00

younger women are also embracing check diving with a passion. We can earn mileage toward free air travel by putting entire restaurant bills on our cards and then having each dining companion reimburse us in cash for their portion. Without technically treating our friends to dinner, we get one step closer to free round-trip tickets.

It was for this very reason that I charged enough group

meals to earn the title of 1995 Northeast Division Check
Diving Champion:

04/08/95	NICOLE'S	FOOD/BEV	162.37
04/09/95	TRATTORIA ALBA	FOOD/BEV	66.00
06/16/95	MATSUSHISA RESTAURANT	FOOD/BEV	242.43
07/05/95	CHINOIS	FOOD & BEVERAGE	224.45
12/13/95	CENTURY CAFE	FOOD & BEVERAGE	145.27

Mileage is the only logical explanation for how I could have
bought literally thousands of dollars of food that year and
never once made a purchase at Lane Bryant.

As with any dive, the key to a successful check dive is to
make it appear smooth, swift, and effortless. All that should
be required is one fluid movement of the hand, perhaps even
before the check makes contact with the table. In my case, I
had the home advantage whenever I went to the Tivoli
Diner:

06/11/96	TIVOLI	FOOD AND BEVERAGE	25.00
06/17/96	TIVOLI	FOOD AND BEVERAGE	41.14
07/01/96	TIVOLI	FOOD AND BEVERAGE	17.40

Here I knew that, no matter who had joined me for the meal,
Gus the waiter would automatically slap the check down at
my place.
    I've also had luck with the ocular dive, a look and a nod
to the waitperson, which, when mastered, assures the check

will never hover in that vague position in the middle of the table.

Once the check is safely in your hand, the trick is to give an it's-no-big-deal look and say—as if you'd just thought of it on the spot—*Hey, why don't I just put this on my card and you guys can give me cash?* This is enough of a question to seem like you're not taking the mileage opportunity by force, yet it's almost rhetorical, making it highly unlikely that anyone will answer with a no. The rules of fair play in check diving, however, dictate that you must pause for at least two beats to give any dissenters a chance to speak. When it's fully mastered, you'll be able to pull off this question as effectively as a minister at a wedding saying "speak now or forever hold your peace." Nobody *ever* speaks, yet they're all under the illusion that they've been given the chance.

An Unequal Relationship

It's common wisdom that a woman should never arrive at a singles event looking too hungry or desperate. So before I went to the singles fundraiser for a well-known Jewish charity, I decided to at least take care of the hungry part.

12/10/94 LIVE BAIT	FOOD/BEVERAGE	13.11

Not only did Live Bait serve up comfort food with attitude—they had a sign that said: IF YOU WANT HOME COOKING, STAY HOME—the bar was comfortable enough for me to sit at alone without attracting sympathetic glances from people who might imagine I was drowning friendless sorrows rather than just heeding the call of a turkey burger. Live Bait also had the added convenience of a location diagonally across the street from the Toy Building, the venue for the party.

After finishing off the burger, I made my way across the street, where, just past the entrance to the Toy Building, I noticed a very appropriate decorative touch—a jumbo Ken doll.

When it reached down briefly to adjust its balls, I realized that he was not the Ken doll of my childhood. In fact,

"Ken's" name was actually Gary Marklitz, and he was a living, breathing international real estate developer.

Gary's jet-black Ken-doll hair and straight, white Ken-doll teeth all rested on a perfectly proportioned six-footish body. On this particular night, after escaping from the office without time to change out of my too-stiff blazer or to defrizz my hair, I was feeling very undoll-like, but I tried to convince myself that I was Jewish Singles Barbie. I hoped that Gary would be one of those rare guys who actually prefer my unblowdried hair, which some have called "kinky," a term that I'm sure contains an element of wishful thinking.

When I threw him the very open-ended, "So, what's your story?" Gary mechanically recited his résumé: "After I graduated from Dartmouth, I spent two years at the largest development firm in London—just long enough to get a promotion, and to realize I'd rather be a big fish in a pond of my own making than a minnow in some Trump-like megafirm. I contacted my old roommate from Dartmouth, and we put together a business plan for what basically was an international version of a Florida timeshare concept. Unfortunately, the year after revenue shot up forty percent, my partner and I realized we didn't share the same vision and parted ways amicably, at which point I decided to go it alone and launched my own firm called *blah, blah, blah, Inc. and blah blah blah* . . ."

Okay, so Gary was more robot than doll, but experience had shown me that even the warmest, mellowest guys could slip into Interview Mode when they were feeling that initial pressure to impress. I was tempted to slip into the Mode right along with him—to ask about his strengths and weaknesses, where he saw himself in five years, and whether his exes would give references—but that would have to wait.

For now, I gave him my number, a clear sign that I was interested in a second interview.

Guys want you to share their enthusiasm for whatever their passions happen to be. With Gary, they were Steely Dan, lobster, and skiing.

After a few months of dating—happy months, when I got to know Gary as a weekday workaholic who became appealingly laid-back and affectionate on weekends—I found the Steely Dan part easy enough to deal with. Listening to "Rikki Don't Lose That Number" is a fairly benign, if not thrilling, activity.

And even eating lobster was no trouble at all. Unlike with skiing, I didn't have to go shopping for special lobster-wear or commit to spending a week at a Crustacean Resort—and, really, what were the chances I'd be in a cast for a month, explaining, "I broke my leg eating shellfish"?

Which brings us to the skiing, the sore spot in my relationship with Gary.

I never had any desire to ski, mostly because I never had any desire to break a leg, arm, or anything else the handyman in my building couldn't fix for a neatly folded twenty. It didn't help that my mother enjoyed telling me the cautionary tale of her friend Phyllis's daughter, whose two days in Alta, Utah, were followed by six months in traction.

Sure, I loved the idea of hanging out at a snow-covered mountain resort and embracing my inner Heidi, but I never would have decided on a ski trip that involved actual skiing if I hadn't spent weeks listening to Gary begging me to go. And I made it perfectly clear to him that I was only going because I knew *he* would enjoy it so much.

I should have known not to be so accommodating because, as usual, just when I was starting to feel really good about the relationship, things unexpectedly, suddenly, started to sour. I wish guys came with a freshness dating stamp, so at least I could see it coming. I would've saved myself a lot of trouble and money if I'd said, while things were still good, "Gary, I really like you, but I'm afraid I'm going to have to get rid of you because January ninth is your expiration date."

But I didn't. Instead, I went to the Alta ski resort with a well-to-do guy who owned a ritzy condo overlooking Central Park, a weekend house right on the beach at East Hampton, and, I suspect, a fairly hefty stock portfolio.

I should've gotten my first clue of what was to come when, right after landing in Salt Lake City, we went straight to the car rental place, and Gary sweet-talked me into giving them my charge card. "Shoot, I left my card at home," he claimed. "Why don't you give them your Amex just to hold, and then I'll settle it in cash when we bring the car back":

03/27/95 HERTZ	RENT-A-CAR	247.09

The next day, when, even with my fleece-lined boots and thermal socks, I got cold feet about getting on skis and suggested I just sip hot cocoa and relax in the lodge, Gary became more insistent than ever. "You're acting like an old lady," he chided me. "Even my eighty-five-year-old grandmother skis, and she can barely walk."

Hoping the only injury I'd go home with would be a sore arm from all his twisting, I agreed to give it a try and we headed to the ski-rental place. I was less than charmed by Gary's generosity when the lady at the desk outright asked him for his credit card, to which he replied, "She has a very nice job. She can pay for it herself."

03/28/95 **MOUNTAIN RENTAL EQUIP**   **SKIS**   17.00

Gary walked me to my beginners' class on the bunny slopes.

03/28/95 **SKI SCHOOL**   **INSTRUCTION**   38.00

He wished me luck and headed off to conquer the diamond trails.

Just ten minutes into my half-hour class, I was shocked to find myself effortlessly gliding down the slope, feeling more like a soaring dove than a bunny, with a form and balance so natural, the teacher shouted "Good!"—not *very* good and not *great*, but a plain, unadorned "good," which was more than enough of an accolade for someone who hadn't learned to ride a two-wheeler until she was eleven. As the only bunny skier singled out for special praise, I finished the lesson feeling like the valedictorian of my beginners' class. Sure, the entire class consisted of a sixtyish Japanese man with iced-up Coke bottle glasses and me, but I was proud to excel nonetheless.

However, I hadn't found the skiing nearly thrilling enough to offset the bother of trudging to the slope and back in twenty tons of skiwear. And, mummified in layer upon layer of clothing, I didn't at all enjoy the very oxymoronic experience of sweating like a pig while surrounded by snow.

Back at the lodge, I found Gary lounging by the fireplace in the lobby, wearing a confident I-told-you-you'd-love-it grin. "So?" he said. "Are you ready to hit the diamond trail?"

"Maybe the cubic zirconia," I quipped. "I did way better than I thought I would," I said, an honest answer, since I'd been sure I would end up dead or a paraplegic, and, so far as I could tell, I still had a pulse and full use of both of my legs.

"So did you love it? Are you hooked?" he asked, obviously craving an enthusiasm I couldn't muster. I had just been asked the skiing equivalent of "Did you come?" when I in fact had not.

I wasn't going to fake an orgasm in bed, and I definitely wasn't about to fake one in the lobby of a ski lodge. "I'm glad I tried it," I said, sounding upbeat if not elated.

That night I was under some weird illusion that I would be Gary's date for a lovely dinner. But thanks to Gary's old college pal Chet, who joined us at the restaurant in Salt Lake City, I ended up being a fly on the wall for Boys' Night Out.

I watched as the boys relived their fraternity days, two carefree bachelors flirting with the hostess. "We're from New York," Gary said, with a tone so arrogant, he must've fully expected she'd go screaming, "OH MY GOD, WE HAVE A GENUINE NEW YORKER HERE!!!! MIMI! KAREN! COME QUICK SO WE CAN GET HIS AUTOGRAPH!"

Her actual response sounded to my ear more like, "Oh. So did you guys want a booth or would you like that table by the window?"

Gary looked at me: "It's your call."

"By the window's fine," I said, relieved that the table was beyond flirting distance from the hostess's podium.

I wasn't sure whether it was my lukewarm response to losing my skiing virginity or the mere fact that Gary was in the presence of a single guy friend that led to his single guy behavior, but I'd never before seen a guy on a date be quite so picky-uppy.

"Which are you," he asked the tall, redheaded, gently freckled, ivory girl who came to take our orders, "an actress or a model?"

I was totally humiliated, as much by the cheesiness of his line as by his flirting so overtly while I was four inches away.

With a quick "Neither, but thanks," she efficiently got the conversation back on message:

"Our special tonight is penne pasta with a bolognese sauce, our appetizer is hearts of palm, and we're also offering an orange-almond salad with fresh oranges over Romaine lettuce, topped with grated almonds and balsamic vinaigrette."

"Love the shoes," Gary said, as his eyes took the slow route along her calves to rest uncomfortably long on heels that looked way too high for a woman who would be balancing heavy plates of china.

"Whoa, she's got some pretty good heels on there," Chet added, clearly salivating more from the waitress than at the thought of the penne bolognese. I looked at my own low-heeled boots, a choice dictated by the very limited range of styles available for my quadruple-A width feet.

After our high-heeled waitress took our orders and disappeared, Gary turned to Chet and asked, "How tall do you think she is? I'm thinking she's a good five-nine."

"Five-eight, tops," Chet said. "And then three feet that way," he added, tackily gesturing toward his nonexistent mammaries.

"What's *your* guess?" Gary asked, suddenly the host of a game show on which I had not realized I'd be the new challenger.

With too much pride to admit I was jealous or even slightly hurt, I played to win: "She looks like she's five-nine, but if you factor in the vertical stripes on her pinafore and the heels," I reasoned, "she's probably a few inches shorter than she looks, so I'd say five-six."

"Okay, I'll ask her when she comes back," Gary said, "and whoever comes closest gets a free drink."

Free drink? I thought. *What about an entree? Some pie?* Come to think of it, after having spent a small fortune on ski gear and putting up with his flirting, wasn't I entitled to a whole showcase of fabulous prizes?

"So how tall are you?" he asked the waitress, who was temporarily four-eleven as she bent forward to set the entrees on the table.

"A little over five-six," she answered mechanically, followed by an all-business "Would you like some fresh pepper?"

"Okay." Gary looked at the napkin where he'd jotted down our guesses. "You came closest, Amy, so dinner's my treat."

Amazing—without even competing in a bonus round, my prize was upped from a beverage to an entire three-course meal! Was Gary totally zonked from his dark ale? Or was there a little shred of hope that he was beginning to re-turn to his pre-Alta, fairly generous self?

One hour later we were back at the hotel parking lot and Gary chivalrously darted around the car to open my door. "Thanks for dinner. That was nice," I said, attempting to put my bitterness into temporary storage and settle in for a snuggly, snowy night.

"My pleasure," he said, "and I mean that, really. Just that you came and even *tried* skiing means so much to me."

Hmm, I thought, *maybe we're making some progress here,* as Gary handed me a smallish cardboard box. Though it was too big for jewelry and wasn't wrapped in paper or tied up with a ribbon, I took the fact that he was *giving* me some-thing as a step in the right direction.

"You should probably open it in the room," he said. "It's pretty fragile."

Heeding his advice, I waited until we were seated on the slightly soiled loveseat in our budget motel room to slowly and carefully unhook the cardboard tab from the little slit on the box top. Gently taking off a couple of layers of bright pink tissue paper, I revealed a ceramic coffee mug with a gi-ant snowflake and the word "Alta" emblazoned on it.

Speechless, I paused and eked out an honest, "I don't know what to say." Not only do I rarely drink from mugs, but it looked suspiciously like the same one that came free with the hot cider Gary had ordered in the bar just nights before.

"You deserve it, and more," he said sweetly, "especially

since, well, you know how much I appreciate that you're covering the rental car."

"What?" I asked. "Are you insane? I never agreed to that. The only reason I gave the car rental place my charge card was because you said you forgot to bring yours and would reimburse me in cash!"

"I don't remember saying that," he argued. "And anyway, the bottom line is, I'm going through a lot more cash here than I thought. With all my partnership stuff up in the air, I can't be spending money like water. I would think you'd be a little more understanding."

"Well, if you couldn't afford to go, you never should have talked me into coming," I countered.

After a few intense rounds of who paid how much for what and who should've paid and who owed whom how much, I began to see the wisdom of the adage that you never really know someone until you go on a trip with them—and I had to consider myself lucky that, in this case, the trip wasn't our honeymoon.

Once we got back to New York, I was totally shocked that Gary kept calling as usual, as if everything were fine and nothing had changed.

"We need to talk," I said, using what I thought was the universal code for This Isn't Working.

Apparently Gary was not of this universe. "Okay, then let's have dinner somewhere on the quiet side. I'm in the mood for Italian," he said, with a cheeriness that hinted at his blissful ignorance of the chat to come. "Why don't I take you to Notaro?" he suggested.

"That'd be fine." I figured the cozy neighborhood Italian place would be as good a place as any to end things.

04/07/95 NOTARO	FOOD & BEVERAGE	43.95

Looking back, I can honestly say that the time Gary took me to Notaro was the best $43.95 I ever spent.

Unwelcome Visitors

If there's one thing you learn as you start to make your way in the Real World, it's that you can't control everything. You can't always control what happens at your job, you can't control who falls in love with you and who doesn't, and you can't control whether it'll be a good hair day or a lousy one.

But nothing exemplifies that which we can't control more than when your apartment is taken over by a family of cockroaches.

I *assume* they were a family because I saw two fairly large roaches and what looked like a couple of babies, though, come to think of it, neither of the big ones was wearing a wedding band. They could've selected my apartment for a roaches singles party, I guess.

When roaches come to visit, they do not announce themselves to the doorman, ring your doorbell, or call you up, asking, "Hey, Amy, I was gonna be in New York for a few days and was wondering if I could crash at your place. No, don't be silly, I don't need a bed—I can sleep in the crevice behind your stovepipe."

Which is how I ended up at the hardware store, investing in a couple of boxes of Roach Motels on the advice of the salesguy, who swore they were the most effective, fume-free way to send cockroaches an eviction notice.

10/28/91 VERCESI HARDWARE	11.89

Personally, I'd always been skeptical of the whole concept: if I'm trying to reduce the roach population, why set them up in their own hotel room, a place that encourages them to reproduce? I might as well throw in a bottle of champagne, some Barry White CDs, and some roach pornos like *Deep Antenna* or *Debbie Does Behind the Kitchen Cabinets*.

But since bugs completely gross me out, I was willing to give it a try and become chief proprietor of an entire chain of Roach Motels, with eight inconvenient locations.

I stuck the boxes in the moist areas beneath the kitchen sink, in the deepest recesses of the bathroom vanity, in the dark space between my fridge and the stove, and, in a shrewd attempt to think like a roach, I slid one right under a package of store-bought fudge brownies.

Just as I was about to announce the grand opening of my newest location—within easy crawling distance of both the toilet and the bathtub—a five-inch-long Godzilla-like roach went strutting across the bathroom wall.

Squinting my eyes just enough so I could track Roachzilla's whereabouts without actually seeing him in all his skeevy detail, I was paralyzed with fear, certain that it would be just a matter of moments until he was crawling up my arm or, worse yet, making a home in my roach-brown hair, which would make it doubly hard to find him.

And then the phone rang. It was Eric, the puppy-dog-eyed struggling actor I'd dated nearly half a year ago, who as luck would have it lived just two blocks away.

"Oh, my God, I'm sooo glad you called," I said, excitedly. "Can you come over now? Pleaaassseeeee," I begged.

"You really miss me, huh?" he said, sounding pleased that I had not yet found an appropriate understudy.

"I just saw a roach the size of Godzilla!!!" I screamed. "Please come kill it!!!!"

"Oh," his voice dropped with disappointment. "I just got in from an audition and I'm exhausted. Can I do it tomorrow?"

"Tomorrow?" I said. "The roach'll be gone by tomorrow!!!"

"Well, then, where's the problem?" he said, with a logic I guess you'd have to be a guy to understand.

The Job Loss Curse, and My Paris Adventure

Call me traditional, but if I'm dating someone, I think there are still certain things the guy should pay for.

For example, his rent.

For reasons I haven't yet figured out, 1996—a time of instant Internet zillionaires and Wall Street wunderkinds—was for me The Year of the Struggling and Unemployed Guy. Every man I met either had just lost his job or would lose his job within weeks of meeting me. Even Steve, the self-employed dentist—how was it even possible for a self-employed dentist to get laid off?—within weeks of our first date, lost his license due to some insurance-fraud thing.

With my own job as an ad-agency copywriter apparently intact, I started to suspect I might be a carrier of The Job Loss Curse. This raised the ethical issue of whether I had a responsibility to warn my dates, so they could brown-nose their superiors or take other protective measures.

My suspicions that I was a carrier were confirmed when Phil, the graphic designer I'd met at an ATM, broke down in tears at a restaurant on our first date, explaining that, just hours earlier, he had gotten a call from a coworker tipping him off that the ax was scheduled to fall on his head the next morning.

Though I usually don't fall for clever pickup lines like "If I don't find a job by February, I'm gonna hang myself," or "Can you lend me a fifty?" I really don't have a problem dating a guy who's temporarily out of work. The sad truth is, all of the above-mentioned men dumped *me*. The ones who offered reasons said they just didn't feel like relationship material right now, or that they wanted to focus all their energies on finding a job and were just looking for "casual fun." The guys who got laid off, it seemed, weren't looking for anything more than getting laid and getting off.

It was around this time that I got a phone message from my mother: "Hi, Amila. Rose Manowitz told me that the Concord resort is having a singles weekend, so I thought it's something you may want to consider." The Concord, a classic Catskill mountain resort like the one in the movie *Dirty Dancing*, always struck me as the kind of place that would draw the nerdy and desperate singles. Mom continued, "At least that way, if a guy doesn't take a shine to you right away, you've got from Friday till Sunday to see if you can *float his boat*."

"So my mother said we should try and meet guys at the Concord," I said the next day—with a can-you-believe-this-lousy-idea eye roll—to my friend Jana, another single woman at the ad agency.

Considering Jana is an edgy girl without a nerdy bone in her body, I found her response nothing short of shocking: "I think it's a great idea," she said.

"You're kidding."

"No, why not? Any guy who takes the Concorde has got to be well traveled, and if he's paying thousands of bucks just to shave a few hours off his flight, you know he's not going to be hitting you up for lunch money."

With an unintended twist of words, we'd hatched a plan that began with my call to Air France's reservations line to purchase a fully refundable one-way ticket to Paris on the world-renowned Concorde, for a flight we had absolutely no intention of taking.

04/07/96 AIR FRANCE	CONCORDE	5,124.00

We did, however, have every intention of nibbling on the complimentary caviar and crackers and sipping champagne as we mingled with the single male jet-setters we were sure would be in the exclusive Concorde departure lounge. Then we'd make a last-minute dash to the ticket counter for a refund.

The next day, with an American Tourister carry-on on my shoulder, a matching tote, and a *Frommer's Guide to Paris* in my hand, I waved down a yellow cab. The driver emerged from the taxi to help me with my bags, but I shooed him away—I was confident I had the strength and muscle tone to hoist two completely empty leather bags into the backseat.

Zipping quickly up twenty blocks, we stopped in front of a beige-brick canopied building to pick up Jana.

"So where you girls goin'?" the driver asked.

"Paris," we both answered, seizing our opportunity for a pre-scam dress rehearsal.

"Business?" he probed.

"Yeah, we're in advertising," I told him. "We're meeting with a perfume company."

"I figured it was business." He was obviously proud of his people sense. "I got a nose for stuff like this after driving for thirty years." I was liking this cabbie and truly hoped we'd reach the airport soon, so my curse and I could get out of his cab and he could make it to thirty-one years.

Upon arriving at JFK Airport, we found our way to the Concorde lounge, and my competitive instincts took over. I quickly scanned the crowd to get first dibs on the best guys, relying on my gut to ferret out the locals from the homeward-bound Frenchmen.

Immediately I realized there wouldn't be a whole lot of ferreting going on. There were only six other people in the waiting area: a couple who appeared to be in their seventies, two ivory-haired Betty White look-alikes, an eighty-something professor type, and a youngish man—probably his nurse—cutting up and feeding him the already bite-size cucumber sandwiches.

I didn't know whether to start a conversation or a bingo game.

Glancing at my watch, I was encouraged to see that there were still forty minutes left to departure, more than enough time for the lounge to fill up with young, vital jet-setters. And as I glanced back up, two fortyish guys appeared seemingly from out of nowhere, each carrying a briefcase but looking otherwise more like tourists than international deal makers.

The shorter, dark, Italian-looking guy gave me the once-over, assessing my proportions as if I were a carry-on and he needed to know whether I'd fit under the seat in front of him or in the overhead bin.

"Hi, I'm Cal," he said, extending a hand first to me, then to Jana. His left one, I noticed, was ringless.

Then his tall, Nordic-blond friend diplomatically smiled at us both, showing favoritism to neither, though I thought he was more Jana's type than mine—until, after the requisite Where're-you-from/Where're-you-goings, he let slip one crucial detail: "I want to be back in the city by the twelfth, because Ringling Brothers leaves town that Sunday, and I make it a point to catch the circus every year."

I absolutely love the circus. If it didn't imply that I had three heads or a beard, I would go so far as to say that I am a circus freak. I've dated guys who are not circus people and guys who are circus people, and I've always gotten along better with the circus people. And if they're unpretentious enough to prefer the traditional Ringling Brothers over circuses with fancy French names and no elephants, all the better.

Realizing that a shared love of three rings did not necessarily mean he'd be giving me a fourth, I also learned that he was a pediatrician who lived on Thirty-second Street—a block and a half from my apartment—and that he frequented Lan Ting, my favorite Chinese restaurant. So I was surprised when it wasn't The Nordic Blond Guy but Cal who made an overture toward a rendezvous in Paris. "Give us the number where you guys are staying. We'd love to take you to dinner," he offered, "though it'll have to be after Thursday."

"Yeah," The Nordic Blond Guy affirmed, "Thursday's our commitment ceremony."

Great. We actually met two decent guys willing to make a commitment, and it was to each other.

As they announced the first boarding call, I was more than ready for departure. Leaving Jana to inhale one more finger sandwich, I darted to a pay phone behind a gray metal partition just a few yards from the check-in desk and dialed a customer service agent for the Concorde. In my best upper-crust, pseudo-British accent, I implored, "Would you *please* be kind enough to page Amy Borkowsky and Jana Greene and tell them there's been an emergency at their office and they are *not* to board the flight to Paris. Tell them they are to return to the office *immediately.*"

Air France obviously knew a thing or two about the speed of sound. I had barely hung up the phone when the page resounded throughout the boarding area: *Amy Borkowsky and Jana Greene, please contact the gate agent for an urgent message. Amy Borkowsky and Jana Greene, check with the gate agent for an urgent message.*

Presenting ourselves to the neatly pressed woman at the counter, we feigned surprise and disappointment at having our first business trip to Paris canceled.

"I was so looking forward to seeing the Chanel factory," Jana lamented.

"And the McDonald's on the Champs-Elysées," I added, not wanting to give the impression that we didn't need our five grand back.

04/07/96 AIR FRANCE   CONCORDE   −5,124.00 (CREDIT)

The Sweater Dilemma

There's no tougher dating dilemma than when you're seeing a guy who's five foot five and a hundred thirty pounds, and you want to buy him a sweater for the holidays.

"He'd definitely be a small," said the basketball-player-tall salesguy at Macy's after hearing Josh's vital stats.

"Definitely do *not* get him a small," advised my average-height friend Danny. "No guy wants to admit he's a small. If you give him a small it's an insult."

I asked Todd, an old friend from college and the only guy I personally knew who was five-three. "Most short guys are in complete denial about being short," he said, "so you better get him the medium or it could freak him out. But I wouldn't just go with my opinion on it—I'm five-seven."

I went back to Macy's, and the salesguy, who looked like he hadn't been five foot five since he was ten, advised, "Look, I could sell you the medium, but I'm warning you—he's going to be swimming in it, and he's going to have to bring it right back to the store. And it's a hundred percent wool, which stretches, so small is really the way to go."

Comforted by Macy's liberal return policy, I decided to

buy both the small and the medium and continue my re-search.

I asked my neighbor, Sue, whose husband is five-six. Sue is a trained psychotherapist and would at least understand that it wasn't just about practicality.

"At this stage, he's still looking to impress you," she assessed, "and he may be going through a lot of anxiety about the short thing. I would just give him the medium with the receipt, so he can exchange it himself. That way he ends up with a sweater that fits, and he feels okay about it since he thinks that you think he's a medium."

I was shocked. Was a psychologically enlightened professional really telling me that a short guy's ego is *that* fragile? In that case, should I just cut out the tag and present the sweater to him in a bag from the Big Man Tall Man shop? Should I buy him an extra large—but not tell him it's from the Boys' Department?

The following day I stopped in at Starbucks and grabbed a sandwich and the smallest cup of coffee they make.

They call this smallest size a Tall.

I thought, *the men's clothing makers could learn a lesson from Starbucks.*

I felt brilliant for having made this observation, until I called Ellie, who's a total Starbucks fanatic. "If you just look at the menu, yeah, Tall is the smallest size," she informed me, "but there's an even smaller size called a Short, only they don't list it anywhere, and they won't tell you about it. You have to know to ask for it."

What? Was "short" such a dirty word that it couldn't even be listed on the menu in a coffeehouse? If they have to hide the fact that a cup of coffee, an inanimate substance, is short, I could only imagine the pressure that a short, male human being must feel.

I wondered, will our culture ever advance to where Short 'n Small Men's Shops will spring up in every mall, and a man of small stature can proudly proclaim "I wear a petite!"? Probably not, but couldn't they at least take a cue from the car companies and come out with a size for guys called compact?

I don't consider myself to be an activist type of person. I've never written a letter to my congressman or worn a "Save the Whales" button. Every now and then, though, I encounter a cause about which I am so passionate, I simply must take a stand.

Since I'm not the type to establish the American Committee Against Size-ism or to march through the streets of Washington chanting "Equal rights for guys of all heights!" I staged my own subtle but clear rebellion: I schlepped back to Macy's and returned the medium.

12/10/96 MACY'S   MEN'S APPAREL   −48.06

By the time Saturday night rolled around and Josh was at my

place, I'd gained some perspective and realized that I'd made an unnecessarily big deal over a small sweater. Since this was our first holiday season together, he'd no doubt be thrilled that I'd gotten him anything at all.

As I handed Josh the bright-red Macy's box with the festive white ribbon, he gave me an appreciative smile. "Okay, so I know it's something to wear," he surmised. Then, slowly and carefully, he peeled off the wrapping and removed the navy-blue cable-knit sweater.

Holding the arms out to view the gift in all its glory, his expression turned to one of grave concern as he asked, "What size did you get?"

"A small," I said, quite nondefensively.

"It probably won't fit," he warned me. "I usually take a medium."

"Well, the salesguy said that since it's one hundred percent wool, it could stretch."

"Maybe," he allowed, "but I almost always take a medium."

"Why don't you try it on, and if it's not right, I'll return it," I suggested.

I went to rummage through my backpack to find the receipt, and when I returned, I saw that, in fact, the sweater did not fit.

The arms were hanging almost to the floor, and standing before me was a navy-blue cable-knit wool chimpanzee.

I was dating a guy who was smaller than small.

"Where'd you buy this?" he asked. "The size is way off."

"Macy's," I told him.

"This is so weird, because their stuff usually fits," he said, genuinely puzzled. "Maybe the guy was right and it stretched."

I noticed that not only was the size of the sweater off, but there was a deep crease in each of the arms. "Let me see this," I said, examining it more closely.

"It must be irregular or something," he said, and I wasn't quite clear on whether he was referring to the sweater or his arm.

"I figured it out," I said, happy to be the bearer of such fabulous news. "The sleeves are supposed to be folded up along this line here, so you have a cuff thing going on. See?" I asked, folding back a good three inches of overhang.

"A cuff thing," he repeated, relieved to now possess perfectly fitting sleeves. "I knew it. I knew something wasn't right. But look what's happening now."

"What?"

"When you fold up the cuffs, part of my wrist is sticking out. I just don't think this sweater is right. Do you have the receipt so I can get something else?"

"Sure," I agreed. "Would you rather have a scarf?"

"That's okay," he said, and paused for a moment. "I think I'll just exchange it for a medium."

I was left with the insight that size really does matter, not to mention a newfound appreciation for the fact that condoms are one-size-fits-all.

In Pursuit of a Couch

I had just moved into the first apartment I would ever live in by myself, and a new couch, the centerpiece of any living room, had become the number-one item on my shopping list.

Keep in mind that this was before people commonly found second-hand stuff online. Which doesn't seem right to me, even now. While I can see how it might be nice to own a sofa that's an heirloom from your Aunt Stella, there's just not the same level of pride in saying, "This sofa was handed down from suckmyweenie193."

No, I was going to buy a brand-new couch—one that would really make the statement that this was a Home, worthy of a decent piece of furniture, rather than just a weigh station until a husband or live-in boyfriend came along. I would choose the color, style, and fabric by myself, pay for it by myself, and—if my luck in the romance department didn't pick up—sit on it by myself. It would be my own upholstered, polyurethane-filled Declaration of Independence.

And so, for nearly two months, I spent lunchtimes and Saturdays combing every furniture store in Manhattan, in search of the perfect couch.

After looking at what must've been a couple of hundred different models—from compact love seats to queen-size sleepers, from silky, soft fabrics to tough, grainy leathers—the first couch that I truly fell in love with was a pastel floral print:

07/06/91 K.J. URBAN DESIGN   FURNITURE   863.00

During the time between the purchase and the actual delivery, however, it dawned on me that the one stain I see most often in my living space is bright-red lipstick. Because I'm constantly applying and reapplying it, I find the red marks everywhere, and not just in obvious places like on my sheets and towels. I have no idea how, but tiny specks of it end up on my fridge door, my walls, my floors. And my old roommate used to complain that she was always discovering my lipstick marks on her off-white fabric sofa.

Realizing that if my new couch weren't lipstick resistant I'd never be able to totally relax on it, I decided to put my pastel floral fabric swatch to the test. Feeling only a shade more normal than a guy getting into things with a blow-up doll, I brought the swatch toward my lips and planted a long, passionate kiss right in the center of one of the large, white roses. After giving the lip-shaped stain time to settle into the fabric, I began an all-out cleaning assault, using every weapon from Tide to Woolite to club soda.

Still, the mark clung to the fabric as stubbornly as ever.

You have to kiss a lot of swatches before you find your print, I concluded, and headed back to the store to cancel my order and perhaps pick something more stain resistant.

```
07/11/91 K.J. URBAN DESIGN  FURNITURE  -863.00 (CREDIT)
```

I found the next couch of my dreams in the furniture section
of a department store.

```
08/03/91 BLOOMINGDALE'S      FURNITURE        2,385.25
```

This couch converted to a full-size sleeper and was a tannish
leather that would, I hoped, go with just about any color.
Though the sofa was basic and neutral, I looked forward to
being able to experiment with various brightly hued throw
pillows.

But the next day, when I told my friends and family
about my safe, neutral sleeper sofa, I realized there was a
danger I'd not even considered.

"Great, a sofa *and* a bed," said my friend Alicia in Chicago.
"Next time I'm in New York, I'll have somewhere to stay."

"You know I'm not really into decorating, but if you like
it, that's all that matters," said my friend Danny. "By the way,
my cousin Gina's coming in next month for a job interview—
do you think she can sleep at your place?"

"Oy, it sounds beautiful," said my mother, approvingly.
"Now I'm thinking maybe I won't come to visit next Mother's
Day."

"Why not?" I asked.

"I'll just wait until June and come for the summer."

```
08/08/91 BLOOMINGDALE'S    FURNITURE  -2,385.25 (CREDIT)
```

After spending yet another entire Saturday scouring the city in search of a couch, traipsing from furniture stores to decorator showrooms, department stores to mom'n'pop shops, I just wanted to go home and collapse on my couch. If only I had one.

Why is this so hard? I wondered. It's only a piece of furniture, right? Why couldn't I just pick something and stick with it? Would it be easier if I had someone to argue with, a significant other who'd *insist* on the forest-green tweed, making me realize just how deeply I loved the floral print, stain resistant or not? Was I afraid of spending the money? Afraid of the commitment?

"Maybe you should see a shrink about this," my good friend Ellie suggested. "You've been couch-shopping non-stop for months now, and I'm starting to worry about you."

It's always darkest before the dawn, I told myself and kept the faith that Couch Nirvana was near. After all, couch-shopping was still easier than dating—so far, not one couch had rejected *me*, told me I wasn't its type or that it wasn't ready to move in just yet. Maybe I wasn't used to having so much power, so much choice, and that was the whole problem.

Finally, on yet another Saturday, I walked into Foremost Furniture, and the palest of powder-pink Italian leather sectionals called out my name. With its gently curved, half-moon pillows, it spoke to me: *Comprami e dovrai sbarazzarti di me quando ti sposerai, perché mai nessun uomo veramente eterosessuale potrà vivere con uno sbiadito e sformato divano rosa*—which is Italian for "Buy me and you'll have to dump me when you get married, 'cause no bona fide straight man could live with a powder-pink curvy couch."

This was one calfskin not made for watching the pigskin; if I was going to watch any sport on this couch, it'd have to be figure skating, and I'd be more likely to yell "Please pass the champagne" than "Hand me the remote."

Was it too female? I wondered. Yes, I'd already decided it was for me, regardless of what anyone else might think. But did it make sense to spend almost *three thousand dollars* on a pink couch? What if I got sick of pink one day and wanted to change my color scheme to green or orange or brown?

"It also comes in cream." I looked up and saw that the voice belonged to a salesman, who introduced himself as Norm.

"I'll take it," I said, as I dug through my bag and handed him my charge card:

09/04/91 FOREMOST FURNITURE	2,988.08

"Well, okay, then!" said Norm, who had spent a full fifteen seconds selling me the couch. "You're my quickest sale today, but I guess you're just a woman who knows what she wants!"

Weeks later, when my couch finally arrived and looked *absolutely perfect* in my living room, I realized that all the almost-rights, the close-but-no-cigars, and the it'd-be-perfect-if-onlys don't matter once you find The Right One.

Miss America

I met Jim, an award-winning jingle composer, at a party hosted by the owner of a recording studio that my ad agency worked with. When Jim called me at the office the following day, without even waiting the requisite forty-eight to seventy-two hours, I was pleasantly surprised.

From our very first date, I suspected the chances were slim that I'd ever end up naked with this lanky dark-haired Italian guy, because he used an extremely effective form of birth control. He said to me, "My last girlfriend was a Miss America."

I knew there was no way I could stack up against someone who most likely was a twenty-year-old who was stacked.

"She had such a beautiful voice," he claimed, "that when she sang 'Somewhere Over the Rainbow,' you would've thought Judy Garland had come back from the dead."

Sure, I had my own talents, too, but I feared that Jim wouldn't be impressed if a Miss America emcee announced, "And now, for the talent portion of the competition, Amy Borkowsky will sit at a desk with a cup of coffee and come up with an ad campaign for Birds Eye Frozen Broccoli."

It didn't stop me from trying to get something started,

though. Apart from his genuine sweetness, nearly black curly hair, and smooth olive skin—the kind of look I normally only see in guys I meet on vacation who don't speak English—Jim was something I wasn't. He was the embodiment of Happening. If there was a celebrity-studded party, an art opening, a movie premiere, Jim would be there.

We had a second date the following week, when I eagerly accepted Jim's invitation to have dinner at Planet Hollywood just prior to some music industry event he was attending. I even bought a new blouse for the occasion:

07/07/98 EXPRESS	APPAREL	42.79

I remember the silky sapphire-blue shirt that was fitted enough at the waist to define my figure, yet flowing enough at the top to add fullness where I could use it.

"So what's your ex doing these days?" I asked, slowly pulling a Planet Hollywood french fry to my lips as if it were a fine cigarillo and trying my best to gracefully conceal that I was feeling threatened.

"She's doing something with arranging food donations to Third World countries, working with the UN," he answered. "But enough about her," he said. "We've been over and done with for almost a year."

I took another bite of my turkey burger, certain that stuffing my face at a trendy restaurant would not meet a pageant judge's idea of feeding the hungry.

I guess the truth is that I was too intimidated by Jim and his history of dating gorgeous women—he also mentioned over dessert that he'd once dated a Ford model—that I couldn't relax and just be myself. To be fair to Jim, he wasn't bragging; the information came up naturally. For example, the Ford model subject arose when I ordered chocolate cake and he said it was refreshing to meet a woman who actually ate.

Still, Jim never called again, and I couldn't blame him, since it was hard for me to be Miss Congeniality when all I could think about was that he'd dated Miss America.

When friends later asked me what happened with the jingle guy, I told them that it was just another case of someone not being able to get over an ex-girlfriend.

What I didn't say was that the someone was me.

Misadventures in Ticket Buying

Bruce Springsteen, the Rolling Stones, Madonna—all consistently sell out venues from the London Palladium to Madison Square Garden, inspiring die-hard fans to camp out at ticket booths on pillows of jackets and mattresses of cold, hard cement.

When my alarm went off at 2:45 on the morning of December 16, 1991, I was unaware that such extreme measures wouldn't be necessary to score tickets to see a new, up-and-coming crooner named Harry Connick, Jr.

Having finally, I thought, overcome my nerdy youth—during which my only concert experience was seeing the ageless heartthrob Engelbert Humperdinck with my parents when I was four—I was feeling like the ultimate edgy hipster as I headed out in the still-dark wee hours, accompanied only by a commuter cup of hot Folger's, to join the throngs of other Harry fans who'd gladly exchanged a night of sleep for the opportunity to witness what would no doubt be The Concert of the Century.

As I passed through the lobby, the overnight doorman looked up: "You're up early."

"Yeah," I replied, "I'm going to get tickets to Harry Connick, Jr."

"Happy Chanukah to you, too," he replied, and I wasn't sure if he was making a bad joke or just didn't hear me.

Only steps out the door, I quickly scored a cab. "Madison Square Garden, please," I instructed the driver. "And if you could circle the block to make sure you drop me at the end of the line, I'd appreciate it." The Garden was right next to Penn Station, and the last thing I wanted was to be lost among the undesirables who loitered there nightly. But upon arriving at the Garden's front plaza, I was surprised to see no line. Did I have the day wrong? Or was I mistaken about the venue?

"Can you keep the meter running while I go and see if the line's inside?" I asked, and the driver replied with a begrudging nod.

Sprinting across the vast concrete plaza and up the steps, I reached a wall of multiple glass doors and began trying one after the other, only to find them all locked. A security guard appeared and informed me that, yes, Harry tickets would go on sale today but the doors wouldn't open until seven, and the ticket windows wouldn't open until nine.

Relieved that I'd at least have a uniformed security guy watching over me, I returned to the cab to pay the driver and congratulated myself on beating the masses. I was proud to be, literally, Harry Connick, Jr.'s, Number One Fan in the Greater New York metropolitan area.

Heading back to claim my prime position at the front door, I flipped through my mental Rolodex, trying to determine which of my very closest friends deserved a Harry ticket, knowing that I'd save them perhaps hundreds of dollars in scalper's fees. Surely I'd have to get one for Ellie; sometimes we talked *several* times a day, and if she ever found out I was seeing Harry without her, she would never forgive me. Then there was Sara, who, if she knew I'd offered tickets to Ellie but not to her, would be justifiably pissed—and I certainly couldn't leave out Carolyn, who was always the life of the party. Just to be safe, I decided to buy a couple of extras to hold in reserve, which would have the added benefit of making me The Person With The Tickets, inviting ticketless Harry fans to suck up to me in hopes of snagging a hard-to-come-by seat.

Hours later, with a modest line behind me, I was the first person to step up to the window. "Six tickets to Harry Connick, Jr., please," I said, keeping my voice low, so as not to alert any potential pickpockets to the bounty that would soon be in my handbag:

12/16/91 MADISON SQUARE GARDEN	
PARAMOUNT CONCERT	255.00

As the woman explained where my seats would be, I realized that Harry wasn't technically playing the Garden but the adjoining Paramount Theatre, which seats just over five thousand, instead of twenty thousand. This was good news, since there was now a chance I might actually see Harry's face. And with such relatively limited seating, the law of supply and demand would, I reasoned, make the already coveted tickets even more valuable. I did the math and figured that if I were to resell four of the forty-dollar tickets at ten times their face value and invest the profit in just the right stock, I could be in a very comfortable situation when my future kids were ready for college.

"How on earth can you afford to send Susie to Cambridge?" curious friends would ask.

"Well," I'd explain, "Susie's tuition *and* room and board are covered by the Harry Connick, Jr., Scholarship Fund."

Upon arriving at the office, I immediately hunted down Carolyn, who was at the coffee machine fueling up, and broke the good news that I'd scored her a hot ticket.

She skipped the oh-my-god-I-can't-believe-we're-gonna-see-Harry part and asked the very practical "When is it?"

"Two weeks from Saturday," I told her.

"I'm going to see my cousin in Maine then," she said, "but thanks."

I called Ellie. "I don't really know his stuff, so I'm not a candidate," she said.

I called Sara who, after a series of phone messages, turned down the tickets with a very unambiguous "I'm not into that kind of music. He sounds like Sinatra, and I'm not into him, either."

After extending a few equally ill-received offers to some of my second-tier friends, I tucked the tickets in my dresser drawer, vowing to sell them for top dollar the night of the show, when desperate Harry fans would no doubt be milling about outside the Garden, hoping to luck out with a last-minute ticket.

The night of the concert, I got to Madison Square Garden's Paramount Theatre early in what would prove to be a futile attempt to unload my extra tickets. Implementing my back-up plan, I cabbed it over to the TKTS booth in Times Square, where throngs of tourists grazed for half-price tickets to Broadway shows. Abandoning all hope of a scalping bonanza, I decided I'd be happy to get anything for the tickets—not just to recoup part of my $255, but to recoup my sense of myself as someone who knows what's what, as the young adwoman with her hand, or at least her pinky, on the pulse on what's hot and happening. With less than an hour until showtime, there was only one thing left to do.

I would have a Harry Connick, Jr., Blowout Sale.

Positioned just out of eyeshot of the TKTS window clerk, I eagerly accepted the brochure that a topless-club representative had thrust in front of me and thanked him kindly for the megaphone. Standing in Times Square, I shouted through the rolled-up girlie flyer: "Get your tickets for Harry Connick, Jr.'s, concert tonight! No reasonable offer refused! I'm clearing out my pocketbook to make room for next week's tickets!"

People looked. People smiled. People walked by.

"I will not be undersold!" I continued. "All Harry Connick tickets must go!"

People rushed by. People sauntered by. One Swedish-looking man stopped, but only to snap my picture.

Eventually two couples who were visiting from South Carolina offered me a hundred dollars total for four tickets—a whopping *sixty percent* discount off the box-office price—and, with barely enough time to hop a cab and keep my eight-o'clock date with Harry, I accepted.

"Thanks so much, this is a real treat," said the thirty-five-ish Ron, apparently the leader of the quartet. "Come on, we'll give you a lift over," he said, as he beckoned me into a taxi and then smiled apologetically upon seeing that it would be a tight enough squeeze with just the four of them. "Sorry," he said, and looked as though he meant it.

Too many Harry fans, not enough seats, I noted, and decided that maybe my instincts weren't so off-base, after all.

AUTHOR'S NOTE: Harry Connick, Jr., played to a sold-out crowd that night. A few short years later, I purchased two more Harry Connick, Jr., concert tickets. From a scalper. For two hundred bucks each.

A Married Man

There were times when, after being locked in an office for a week, I needed to see trees, smell grass, and breathe some fresh country air.

There were times when, after being locked in an office for a week, I just wanted to meet a man with whom I'd have the possibility of being locked in a bedroom for a week.

Feeling the need for both nature and nurture during one particularly stressful time at work, I was quite susceptible to the flyer in my mailbox for a Vegetarian Singles Hike that sounded just my speed: "Hike at an easy to moderate pace while meeting other like-minded vegetarian singles."

I'm not a vegetarian, but I figured they'd be a fairly intelligent and enlightened bunch—and, I reasoned, at the very least, it would be one singles event that wouldn't feel like a meat market. I couldn't imagine any woman complaining, "Geez, this place is a real produce stand. Did you see that guy? He looked at me like I was a piece of yellow summer squash!"

To embrace the spirit of the event, I took a bag lunch of a veggie burger and veggie spring roll from a restaurant in my neighborhood.

As it turned out, the group—six crunchy guys who looked to be mostly in their forties and fifties, and three women—was so *non*–meat markety that there wasn't much talking or flirtatious glancing at all. I decided to break the ice with the most provocative question I could think to ask of the only male vegetarian who looked under forty: "So, I was wondering, do vegetarians eat animal crackers?"

After a gee-I-never-thought-about-it look, he answered, "Well, I suppose it would depend on whether they're made with animal fat or vegetable shortening."

"Oh. I was just curious because I'm not actually a vegetarian," I admitted. "The idea of a vegetarian singles hike sounded interesting, though."

"No big deal," he replied. "I'm not actually single."

"So how'd you end up here?" I asked, trying my best to hide my disappointment. "Doesn't your wife like to hike?"

For the next two and a half hours, the vegetarian meathead named Doug literally walked me through his entire marriage, going on and on about the lingerie model-turned-porker who worked neither inside nor outside the home, who could quote verbatim every cover story from *The National Enquirer* but barely knew the name of the president, who was resentful of his parents and his friends, and who always belittled him in public.

Not that he'd ever publicly belittle her, of course.

"You don't know how lucky you are that you're not married," he said. "I'd give my *right ball* to be single again. I swear I would."

And what a catch he would be, with one ball, I thought.

Finally, the group paused near a cluster of bench-sized rocks, and I saw my chance to get away: "It was nice meeting you, Doug, but I think I'm going to pull up a boulder and take a break. Good luck with your marriage, though, I hope everything works out."

"Would it be okay if I called you some time?" he asked.

"Not really, I don't date married men."

I was never one to believe that all the good guys were taken.

But it was nice to know that some of the not-so-good ones were.

A Dating Danny

I was sitting with my platonic male friend, Danny, in our regular haunt, the Tivoli Diner, just a few doors down from his apartment. "What if I never get married, and I get some dreaded disease?" I asked Danny. "Who's going to take care of me?"

"That's a ridiculous worry," Danny dismissed my concerns. Just as I was about to accuse him of being callous and unrealistic, he continued: "It's a ridiculous thing to worry about because if anything ever happens, *I'll take care of you.*"

"You will?" I asked, touched that this busy veterinarian would interrupt a grueling schedule of declawing cats and neutering pigs to nurse a mere platonic female friend back to health.

"Absolutely," he assured me. "You know I'm always here for you."

I wanted to believe it. I really did. After all, Danny was the one I could always count on to listen when I needed to talk, to grab a burger at eleven P.M., when all my girlfriends were in for the night, to give a brutally honest opinion about whether the guy I hadn't heard from since last June was just shy. The sky could fall, lightning could strike, and terrorists could attack, but I was secure in the knowledge that Danny would always be there for me.

In fact, as I would discover, there was one thing that could stop the mighty Danny from rushing to my side: a girlfriend.

Here is a partial list of my American Express charges for dinners with Danny when he wasn't seeing anyone:

05/27/96 TIVOLI	FOOD AND BEVERAGE	8.85
05/30/96 TIVOLI	FOOD AND BEVERAGE	13.49
06/11/96 TIVOLI	FOOD AND BEVERAGE	15.00
06/17/96 TIVOLI	FOOD AND BEVERAGE	11.88
07/01/96 TIVOLI	FOOD AND BEVERAGE	17.40
07/13/96 TIVOLI	FOOD AND BEVERAGE	16.20
08/09/96 TIVOLI	FOOD AND BEVERAGE	10.96

In October 1996, Danny starting dating a young art student named Gabrielle. Here is a complete listing of all my meals with Danny at the diner from October 1996 through when they broke up in November of 1998:

To be fair, Danny did make a couple of attempts for us to all get together. But there was no clearer reminder that Gabrielle was his girlfriend, and that I was just a friend, than when the check would come—he'd ask the waiter to put two thirds on his charge card and a third on mine. And he clearly took his girlfriend to a caliber of restaurant somewhat different from the comfy diner where he used to eat with me:

03/17/97	TAVERN ON THE GREEN	FOOD/BEV	74.86
05/27/98	GIORGIOS OF GRAMERCY	FOOD/BEV	59.10

Gabrielle officially broke up with Danny around New Year's of 1999, and here's what started happening with Danny and me:

01/03/99	TIVOLI	FOOD AND BEVERAGE	8.85
01/05/99	TIVOLI	FOOD AND BEVERAGE	10.75
01/07/99	TIVOLI	FOOD AND BEVERAGE	13.49
01/10/99	TIVOLI	FOOD AND BEVERAGE	15.00

Danny was heartbroken. The breakup was swift, sudden, and he never saw it coming. This was a crisis that would require more than a turkey burger. He needed to talk. He needed someone to listen. In fact, there was one time when, in a single day, Danny had to book two sessions at the Tivoli Center for Psychotherapy:

01/13/99	TIVOLI	FOOD AND BEVERAGE	11.35
01/13/99	TIVOLI	FOOD AND BEVERAGE	14.15

Then one night Danny made a confession. He told me that Gabrielle, who was twenty-one, had teased him about having so many friends who were "over-thirty spinsters" and—though he now regretted it deeply—he had deliberately avoided hanging out with me and his other "elderly" female friends. This didn't sit well with me, so I had no choice but to resign as his therapist.

It took a while, but, eventually, Danny did convince me that he had felt terrible for sacrificing our friendship, and I let myself get sucked right back into the pattern of listening to him obsess about his ex. One day I finally told him, "Danny, I'm sorry you're hurting, I really am, but how long am I going to keep sitting here at the Tivoli listening to you obsess about Gabrielle?"

Shortly thereafter, my American Express statements once again included far fewer charges from dinners with Danny. Obviously, somebody was dating someone.

This time, I'm happy to say, it wasn't Danny.

Fantasies, Fulfilled

Most adults—both well-adjusted ones and nutjobs alike—have dreamed their entire lives of someday owning a particular material object that they believe will be their key to contentment. For some it's a Harley, for others a grand piano, and for still others a cabin in the woods or a beachhouse in Malibu.

For me, it was an Easy Bake Oven.

Every birthday and every Chanukah throughout my childhood I'd *beg* for one, and each year I'd get the same thing. Underwear. Fine for warming buns but totally useless for baking cakes.

I longed to be as content as the little blond girl in the commercial, happily mixing *real* ingredients to make a *real* cake in a *real* oven. And as the years passed, I found my mind still often drifting to the oven. Along with its eternal appeal, there was now another draw for a woman with a gradually slowing metabolism: with the mini proportions of the Easy Bake desserts, I would be able to eat an entire angel-food cake or down a full batch of sugar cookies in one sitting and not end up looking pregnant.

With a decent adult salary, and Easy Bake Ovens selling

for a mere twenty dollars each, I had a discretionary income of *over five hundred* EBOs (Easy Bake Ovens) a year, so what was stopping me? I decided to defer my dream no longer, so my Amex card and I made the fifteen-block pilgrimage to Herald Square and Manhattan's only Toys "R" Us.

Savvy and successful, I would not only have my cake, I would bake it myself in an Easy Bake Oven and eat it, too.

I approached the first red-smocked employee to meet my gaze. I could barely believe it when he said, "The Easy Bake Oven? We're out of stock."

Out of stock? Wasn't The Oven a *staple* of toy stores? In my universe, grocery stores always have milk, drugstores have a constant supply of cotton balls, and toy stores— especially huge Toys "R" Us stores—*always* stock the Easy Bake Oven.

Determined to see for myself, I dragged my broken heart over to the aisle of homemaker-ish toys, and right where the oven should have been was a big, gaping hole.

Dashing off to Woolworth's, I knew victory was at hand when the salesgirl directed me to a fully stocked toy aisle, where, she assured me, my oven awaited. Sure enough, there, right before my very eyes, I saw . . . the Watch-It Bake Oven.

Huh? *Watch-It* Bake? I had never heard of a Watch-It Bake Oven. As it is, the Easy Bake is an imitation of a real oven, which makes the Watch-It Bake an imitation *of an imitation*. The name seems to imply that making desserts is a spectator sport, as if people might gather round the oven to watch Monday Night Bundt Cake: "Get out of the way, Johnny, I'm trying to catch the slo-mo replay of the dough rising!"

No, my dream was grander than just *watching* something

bake. I wanted to measure and mix and stir and beat and frost. I wanted to rotate pans for even baking, poke forks in to test the doneness. I didn't want it to be totally effortless. I just wanted it to be *easy*. After all, the Easy Bake Oven might be the closest this still single, Chinese-takeout-addicted woman would ever come to true cookie-baking domesticity, and I wanted to experience it in the fullest, most authentic way possible.

I plodded onward, to a more intimate neighborhood toy store, all the while knowing that something was wrong with this picture—shouldn't I, an adult woman, have been on an oven hunt for *a little girl*, a daughter at home in flannel footsie pj's who goes to bed and wakes up dreaming of an Easy Bake, as I once did? Maybe this is why people have kids, I thought, so they can give their kids the things and experiences they never had themselves. But where would my quest to fill childhood voids end? Would it be only a matter of time before I bought a Barbie Dream House, got tickets to *Disney on Ice*, and auditioned for the Lakeville School majorettes?

Upon entering the upscale toy shop, I silently mouthed "Easy Bake Oven?" to the girl behind the counter, who was diligently engaged in the crucial task of talking to her boyfriend on company time. With an affirmative nod, she pointed me toward the shelf of girls' toys, where what awaited me was none other than . . . the *I-Can*-Bake Oven. I realized I no longer needed my oven—I could bake a complete seven-layer cake with the steam that was coming out of my ears.

No, I would not settle for anything less than the genuine, bona fide, original Easy Bake Oven, and if I had to take my case to a higher authority, then I was ready. Ovenless but not defeated, I returned home and, without even removing my coat, picked up the phone. "Yes, I need the number for the Kenner Corporation," I said with an urgency normally reserved for 911, not 411. Like a sixth-grader at a spelling bee, I clarifed, "Kenner . . . K-E-N-N-E-R," knowing that even I, persevering and resilient, didn't have the constitution to survive ending up with Connor, Kanner, or some other close-but-no-chocolate-cigar corporation.

Eventually, I reached a too-cheery receptionist who, I learned, did double duty as the Easy Bake Naysayer, as she informed me that it was the end of the season and absolutely *no more ovens* would be shipped. I knew this translated to "somewhere there's an oven with your name on it."

I asked to be transferred to the office of the President, where, at long last, an assistant to the President finally located one Easy Bake Oven at a far-flung Toys "R" Us in Ohio, and she said they'd be happy to send it to my home if I gave them my credit card number:

| 03/15/95 TOYS "R" US | TOYS | 21.55 |

Six long days later, I was in my kitchen, tearing brown shipping paper and twine off my childhood dream and discovering that it was more colorful than I knew: the subtle aqua oven of my memories had been replaced by what appeared to be a hot-pink plastic microwave.

I decided to try out my baking skills on Darren the Computer Guy, on what would be our fifth date.

"Are you hungry?" I asked, in a veiled attempt to recruit him as my Easy Bake guinea pig.

"What do you have?" he inquired.

With a deep womanly pride I had never before experienced, I replied, "I just baked a chocolate layer cake."

"Yum," he said, clearly enticed. "Chocolate layer cake is my favorite."

"Then wait till you see this," I said, momentarily disappearing into the kitchen, then reemerging proudly with my perfectly baked, flawlessly frosted masterpiece. I thrusted it toward him in the Easy Bake Oven's plastic baking pan and uttered a heartfelt "Voilà!"

"*That's* the cake?" he said upon seeing my coaster-size handiwork. "That's not a cake. It looks more like a hockey puck."

"No," I clarified, "it's a real cake. I made it with my Easy Bake Oven."

He threw me a gimme-a-break look, and I could almost see the video playing in his head as he envisioned a meager existence with the Mini Food Maven, a life filled with two-ounce steaks, clams on the quarter-shell, and inch-long hot dogs.

"Let's just order in some fudge cake from the diner," Darren suggested.

So what if he called it a hockey puck, I consoled myself. It was *my* hockey puck, and after decades of longing I had finally gotten a goal.

The Mysterious Headache

I don't know exactly when it started, but almost as far back as I can remember, about once a year or so I've had an intensely painful sensation toward the back of my head that feels like someone's jabbing me with an icepick. It comes on suddenly, and, since it lasts just a few seconds, I had never really worried about it. However, in the mid-nineties, when the attacks began striking every few months and with greater intensity, I made an appointment to see my doctor.

"I've been getting these weird pains in the back of my head," I told Dr. Young, "and I just want to make sure it's not a brain hemorrhage or anything."

"How would you describe the pain?" he probed.

"It's a sudden stabbing pain," I told him, "like someone's jabbing me in the back of the head with an icepick."

After giving me a thorough exam and emitting the appropriate "hmm's" and other thoughtful sound effects to accompany his scholarly hand-on-chin posture, the doctor rendered his diagnosis.

"What you have," he said, "is Icepick Headaches."

"You're kidding, right?" I asked, certain I'd never seen Icepick-Headache tablets at Duane Reade.

"It's fairly common. Basically, all it is," he explained, "is a harmless migraine that mimics the feeling of being stabbed in the head with an icepick. Do you drink a lot of coffee?"

09/30/96 STARBUCKS COFFEE		16.31
10/01/96 STARBUCKS COFFEE		10.31
10/26/96 CHOCK FULL O' NUTS	SPECIALTY ITEMS	3.79
10/28/96 COFFEE CRAZE		2.99
11/01/96 STARBUCKS COFFEE		3.51
11/02/96 STARBUCKS COFFEE		3.89
11/02/96 STARBUCKS COFFEE		3.89
11/03/96 CAFE EUROPA	FOOD/BEV	5.61
11/05/96 STARBUCKS COFFEE		3.89
11/06/96 CAFE EUROPA	FOOD/BEV	6.20
11/06/96 STARBUCKS COFFEE		3.10
11/06/96 STARBUCKS COFFEE		5.56

"Why?" I asked. "Does that cause it?"

"No, but caffeine in any form can aggravate a migraine, so you may want to cut down," he advised.

I got home and my mother was already calling in for a report.

"Everything's okay, Mom," I told her. "The doctor said it's a totally harmless kind of a migraine that feels like you're being stabbed in the head with an icepick."

"Well, I wouldn't call that harmless," she insisted.

"Why not?" I asked, a totally unnecessary question since I knew she was already going to tell me why not, anyway.

"Because what if, God forbid, you're walking alone at

night and someone stabs you in the back of the head with an icepick? How would you know? When you should be yelling, 'Help! Police!' you'll be calmly asking passersby, 'Excuse me, do you have some Tylenol?'"

"The odds of that are one in a zillion," I told her.

"And what if the nut is also a pervert?" she asked.

"Don't worry," I reassured her. "I'll just tell him, 'Not tonight, I have a headache.'"

The Junk Drawer

I've always thought it'd be fascinating to go on an archaeological dig, to burrow through the earth with shovels and pans and sifters to discover long-lost remnants of civilizations past.

I've had to settle for cleaning out my junk drawer.

It's a site that, along with the usual stray paper clips, rubber bands, and toaster warranties, always turns up unexpected finds.

I was particularly intrigued one Sunday morning while excavating my own personal Pompeii. In a little black container was a roll of exposed film with an expiration date of May '92. Since my mother has me convinced that anything from outdated milk to an expired charge card can curdle and send me into gastric spasms, I'm normally a stickler for using things before they go bad. I can pretty safely assume, then, that the pictures themselves were taken long before May '92. But when? And why had I not rushed to develop them like I normally do?

I called my old roommate, Terri. "Maybe it's from when you had me take those shots to send to guys from the personals," she said.

I called Ellie. "I bet they're from your trip to Italy," she guessed.

My mother called me. "Who knows when they're from, but be careful where you develop them, 'cause I once heard that they can copy your face onto someone else's body and sell it to *Hustler*."

"They may come out a little grainy, but they should be okay," the one-hour photo guy told me.

"All right then, give it a try," I said.

"You can pick them up on Thursday after three."

"That's *three* days," I complained. "Isn't this supposed to be a one-hour place?" That's me—I can put something off for years and years, but once I make up my mind to do it, I want it done right away.

"We can rush it through, but since this may need special handling, you're better off waiting for Tamir to do it, and he won't be in until Thursday."

Now, even under normal circumstances, when I know exactly what's on a roll of film because I just shot it yesterday, I still can't wait to get the pictures back. My impatience extends to viewing other peoples' photos, too. I hate it when friends come back from vacation with twenty rolls of pictures and, instead of just handing you the whole stack, peel off one at a time and narrate each individual photo, including details that are meaningless if you've never been to the place: "This is when we went to Hooga Monga and toured the El Poopie Forest—oh, and this is our guide, Heinz, in front of the Blah Blah Blah Blah Museum." I don't want to hurt their feelings, so, halfway through the second roll I usually interject, "Stop! The El Poopie Forest sounds so fabulous, you're gonna give everything away!"

But in this case, I had no choice. Three days passed, and as I returned to what I now call the Seventy-Two-Hour Photo Place, I was thrilled to be greeted with excellent news:

"Tamir was able to print twenty-three shots," the counter guy said.

I gave him my Amex card, and before he could even hand me the form to sign, I tore open the envelope, my hands shaky with anticipation. I flipped through a few pictures, then a few more, and let out an involuntary Seinfeldian cry: "Who *are* these people?"

Tearing through nearly two dozen shots of what looked like an American Gothic–ish couple somewhere in the heartland, I was certain there must have been a mixup. Toward the end of the stack, finally, there were three pictures of a woman I recognized: the Statue of Liberty.

"That's definitely the roll you gave me," the counter guy said, pointing to a microscopic number on the negative that appeared to match up with some numbers scrawled on the envelope. "Those aren't your grandparents?" he asked, pointing to the unknown farmer and his wife posing with a calf by a weathered barn.

"Absolutely not," I insisted. "Grandpa Joe's been dead since 1967, and the only calves Nana has are in orthopedic shoes."

"Well, that's what was on the roll, but if you don't want it, you don't have to pay for it," he offered.

"No, I'll take them," I said, not sure why I wanted to pay fifteen dollars for pictures of total strangers.

04/06/96 ONE-HOUR PHOTO	PHOTO/SUPPLIES	14.94

After all that anticipation, I hated the thought of going home empty-handed, and besides, figuring out the identity of the unknown couple could be an interesting challenge.

My first theory was that the roll had been left behind by my apartment's previous tenants, a group of four businessmen who lived in the suburbs and used the apartment when bad weather, a late night at the office, or, I'm guessing, an extra-marital affair made it more practical for them to sleep in the city. That night, I called Mr. Harris—the only one of the four I'd met personally—and described the couple, but he turned out to be a dead end. "I don't have any relatives who look like that, and it's unlikely my partners do either, because two of them are Japanese and the other's Korean."

I had just hung up the phone when it rang. It was the guy at the Seventy-Two-Hour Photo Place. "I owe you an apology," he said, "because there was a little confusion. The couple that's in your pictures came in today, and they said that when they got back to their hotel room and looked at their pictures, the whole stack had a girl and a guy on what looked like a camping trip in the woods. I just took a look, and I'm pretty sure that it's you and some guy."

If he had been there with a roll of Kodachrome, he'd have captured my face turning the deepest shade of tomato red. How could I have forgotten the snapshots I had taken with Mark the PR Guy on the Labor Day that he took me on my first and only camping trip? They were silly, seminaked portraits of him answering nature's call, only partly obscured by what we'd labeled with a handmade sign, the "Men's Tree"—and, I recalled, there were equally revealing shots of me frolicking by the Women's Tree. Intense thunderstorms and cold winds, coupled with the fact that things between us had been rocky to begin with, made the peeing-by-the-tree photos the only bright spot in a trip that was hellish at best, and we broke up a few days after we got back. I remembered I'd thought the pictures must have been ruined when the camera was rained on, so I'd thrown the film in the drawer and forgotten about it.

I had no idea what other embarrassing shots were on the roll, but I knew that until they were back in my hands, I wouldn't be able be sleep, not to mention run for public office. "Do me a favor," I told the photo guy. "If you could have the envelope ready for me, I'll just swing by in a cab and we can do a little swap, okay?"

"That's fine. They'll be right here at the front," he assured me.

I must confess that, as a souvenir of the experience, I did remove one shot of the unknown couple before giving back the envelope.

I tossed it in my junk drawer.

The Disappearing Lipstick

Have you ever wondered where your lipstick goes when it wears off?

It doesn't fall on the ground—there are literally millions of lipstick-wearing women in New York City, and I've never had to warn a friend, "Watch out! You almost stepped in a pile of DuraGlam Cocoa Frost!"

It doesn't melt into the air. The weather guy never says, "The pollen count is 10.5, with a Matte Finish Lipstick Index of a whopping 9.2."

So where *does* the stuff we apply several times a day go after it leaves our lips? It's not like it's water that can just evaporate . . . it's made of waxes and oils and other pretty substantial stuff.

Well, according to an article I read when my ad agency was trying to win a cosmetics account, the lipstick gets absorbed by your body. The article claimed that when coroners do autopsies, they often find globs of lipstick in the intestines.

Before you get all freaked out and toss your lipstick in the trash, keep in mind that nobody has claimed that lipstick was the *cause* of death—depending on the woman, it could've been her eyeshadow, or perhaps that gunshot wound to her temple.

Still, I didn't like the thought of all that lipstick clinging to my organs. There's a limit to just how long-lasting I want my cosmetics to be.

Luckily, Aveda (the company whose advertising we were hoping to do) has a lipstick made of ingredients that supposedly won't accumulate in the body.

We didn't get the account, but Aveda got a new customer:

10/25/96 AVEDA	BEAUTY SUPPLIES/ACC	51.96
03/08/97 AVEDA	BEAUTY SUPPLIES/ACC	12.99
08/30/97 AVEDA	BEAUTY SUPPLIES/ACC	12.99

I acquired a newfound peace of mind with the knowledge that I'd never be rushed to the Mt. Sinai Emergency Room in excruciating pain only to find out that I'd just passed a lipstick stone.

The Case of
the Missing Panties

07/21/93 AMERICA WEST

BALLY'S LAS VEGAS, JUL29–AUG01 989.00

I wish I could say I was one of those totally uninhibited, die-hard fans who faint when within close proximity of their musical idol. It would be fun to be out of control for a while, and not to freak out about freaking out—to willingly let someone move me to tears or to desperate shrieks, like the teenage girls on the news footage of Beatles concerts. But it's not like me to react that way to any singer—not to Mick Jagger, not to Justin Timberlake, and certainly not to Tom Jones.

My only actual memory of Tom Jones was from when I was a very little girl, when my mother would spontaneously belt out "What's New, Pussycat?" anytime she ran into the black cat that belonged to the Goldmans next door. Nevertheless, when Sara, Ellie, and I managed to parlay the broken toilet in our Vegas hotel room into three front-row seats to his concert—a good hotel like Bally's will do almost anything to keep their guests happy—I'd be lying to say that I wasn't looking forward to seeing him. After all, this was supposed to be our forty-eight-hour retreat from Life As Usual, and if listening to Tom Jones singing "Delilah" wasn't a total break from the norm for me, I didn't know what was.

"What's that for?" I asked Sara, as she grabbed something pink and silky from the dresser drawer and scrunched it into her handbag. "Think Tom Jones'll be so exciting that you'll need a change of panties?"

"It's a tradition to throw panties at a Tom Jones concert," she explained. "So I figured, when at a Tom Jones concert, why not do as the Tom Jones fans do?"

"At this point they're probably hurling Depends," cracked Ellie. "Forget my undies—I'll be amazed if he even gets me to take off my coat and stay a while."

Seizing a prime opportunity to at least go through the motions of being a love-crazed fan, and unwilling to part with any panty that was part of a matching set, I talked my friends into making a pit stop on the way to the show:

07/31/93 VICTORIA'S SECRET   LINGERIE   6.22

Let it be known that on July 31, 1993, I became a Tom Jones fan.

I'm ashamed to admit that when he first appeared on the stage, I was skeptical as to whether such a mature man could inspire anything more than a campy sense of nostalgia. But in time—say, around fifteen seconds—I realized that with his seductively raspy wails, thick curly hair, and a body clearly more stricken with passion than arthritis, Tom Jones was a sex symbol for the ages. When he moaned out the second chorus of "Delilah" and women, some timidly and some

with wild abandon, began standing up to chuck their panties, I felt perfectly natural joining in. And when, surpris-
ingly, Sara and Ellie lost their panty-throwing nerve, I
became their designated thrower, standing tall to add two
more pairs to the hailstorm of lingerie that now filled the
showroom.

The next morning, I woke up with a new feeling of freedom
in my soul, fun in my heart, and one burning question: What
happens to all those panties?

Okay, let's say that, very conservatively, women throw a
total of ten pairs of panties at a typical Tom Jones concert. If
Mr. Jones does two shows per night and performs just over
half of the year, that's roughly *four thousand* pairs of panties
per year.

When you consider that women have been throwing
panties at him since the late sixties—well over twenty-five
years—that's a lifetime total of *one hundred thousand pairs of
panties*.

I'd like to know, where are those panties now?

Is Tom Jones hoarding them, stashing them in an under-
ground bunker so if he ever falls on hard times he can auc-
tion them off at Christie's?

Has he sewn them into a quilt large enough to cover the
quadruple-king-sized bed he no doubt needs to accommodate his groupies?

Has he donated them to the Salvation Army and Goodwill, thereby assuring that no American woman need suffer
panty-deprivation?

Has he shipped them to Third World countries? Put

them in a bank vault in Switzerland? Used them as dust cloths?

Obsessed about where they had ended up, I decided to embark on a mission to get my panties back.

First, I called Bally's, and they connected me to a maintenance supervisor in charge of the after-show cleanup. "I'm sorry," he said, "but we don't have any panties here."

"Were they thrown away?" I asked. "Or are they in some kind of storage facility?"

"I don't have any information about your panties," he insisted, "but you may want to try contacting Tom Jones directly."

"Do you happen to have his number?"

"No, sorry, but maybe you can try and look him up through information."

I thanked him for his brilliant suggestion of calling 411 to ask for the number of a Mr. Jones, and hung up.

Instead, I called a friend of a friend who used to be a secretary to some hotshot entertainment lawyer. After making me swear that I'd never reveal my source, she gave me the name, address, and phone number of Mr. Jones's management company in L.A.

My call was answered by a very businesslike woman who, upon hearing that I was quite curious about my panties, brusquely replied, "I don't have time to deal with such frivolous concerns."

Okay, then, I decided. I would send a letter directly to Tom Jones. I would let him know that, more than a matter of mere curiosity, it was *absolutely critical* that I got my panties back. Here is the letter I sent him:

Mr. Tom Jones
Tom Jones Enterprises
———— Blvd.
Los Angeles, CA

Dear Mr. Jones:

I am writing with the hope that you can help me retrieve a pair of
panties thrown onto the stage in error at your July 31st performance at Bally's in Las Vegas.

While overcome with emotion at the second chorus of "Delilah," I
inadvertently grabbed the wrong pair of panties from my travel
bag. The panties in question were a recently discontinued style from
Victoria's Secret and the only perfect match for my favorite floral-
print bra.

If you would be kind enough to scan your panty files, you will easily recognize my pair by the five (5) petals on each flower in the design. More recent floral prints have all had an even number of
petals—usually four or six—and I am convinced that the five-
petal configuration will someday become a collector's item.

But much more significantly, I should mention that both the bra and
panties were the final gift to me from my late husband, who died of
a coronary attack just forty minutes after presenting me with the
above-described underwear.

Upon receipt of the panties, I will gladly send you a replacement
pair via overnight mail. If you have any favorite colors or styles,

kindly enclose a note stating your preference, and I will do my best to accommodate you.

Thank you for your time and trouble. While I was fully prepared to lose my shirt in Vegas, I was not prepared to sacrifice my panties.

Your friend,

Amy Borkowsky

I'm still waiting for a reply.

Single-ism

01/24/98	CAESARS LAS VEGAS	TICKETS	67.50
01/25/98	FLAMINGO HILTON	LODGING	103.98
01/26/98	MIRAGE BUFFET	LAS VEGAS	14.93

Some years after my panty-throwing adventure, lured by a great rate on an air-and-hotel package, I made another trip to Vegas. But this time I went totally solo. I knew I'd feel perfectly safe as a woman alone because the Las Vegas Strip is always bustling, and to say it's well-lit at any hour of the night would be an understatement.

I found, however, that just because I was okay being on my own there, not everyone else was.

Walking through the lobby of one of Vegas's many new and lavish hotels, I passed a booth covered with photos of a lush-looking condo, its inviting pool fringed with gently bent palm trees. Curious, I approached the woman behind the desk. "Those condos look beautiful. Where are they?" I asked.

"Are you here with your husband?" she replied.

"Excuse me?" I asked, confused. "I just wanted to know where the condos in the picture were located."

"They're time-shares right here in Vegas," she answered, "but to tell you about them, I need your husband to be present."

"I don't have a husband," I answered without apology, and, while initially only curious about the condo, I was now, on principle, *determined* to get the full sales pitch that any self-supporting career woman deserved. "I'm still interested in hearing more about the time-shares, though," I persevered.

"What we do here, honey," she explained slowly, as if talking to a four-year-old, "is we set up tours of the property, and we've found it's a waste to give single women a tour, because unless they happen to be widows, they just can't afford it."

The jacketed man beside her chimed in: "And even if it's a widow with money, a woman will tell you yes one minute and then the next day she backs out of the whole deal, so we found it's just not worth the effort."

I couldn't believe it. I'd thought Elvis impersonators were supposed to be Vegas's only vestige of the fifties. Wasn't I experiencing the textbook definition of discrimination? Or were they shrewdly using reverse psychology, taunting me until I whipped out my checkbook, begging, "Sell me my share of your overpriced property *now* or I'm calling my attorney!"

I picked up a pen from their counter and held it poised like a dagger over the back page of a time-share brochure. "I'd like the name and number of whoever's in charge of this operation," I demanded, sounding frighteningly like my mother, whose stock reply when faced with anything less than a satisfying experience is "Let me speak to the manager." I told myself that this transgression was far more seri-ous than her favorite cause (that expired coupons should be honored due to the leap year) and stood my ground.

"The property managers are based in Florida, and they're very busy," the man said, "but maybe we can help you."

"Did we do something to upset you?" the woman asked, and I realized that she might be dumb enough to be truly baffled.

"I'll look them up through Information," I replied, seeing the corporation's name listed on the cover of their flyer. Reaching into my mental medicine cabinet for a dose of their medicine, I added, "I've found it's a waste of time to dis-cuss my complaints with low-level employees. Unless they happen to be managers, they don't understand, so I found it's just not worth the effort."

The two time-share peons looked at each other as if they'd just seen an alien.

I turned away and strode purposefully toward the slot machines, for which I developed a newfound respect: after a half-hour, they'd taken seventy-five dollars of my money and couldn't have cared less whether or not I had a husband.

AUTHOR'S NOTE: On later trips to Vegas, I've had similar experiences at the time-share booths, and one employee actually showed me a memo on company letterhead that said "No tours for single women." If *60 Min-utes* wants to send me back out there with a hidden camera to do an ex-posé, I'd welcome the chance.

Platonic Male Friends

I had just finished one of those how-to-enjoy-New-York-on-a-shoestring seminars when I noticed a single black leather glove left behind on a desk. "Hey, did anyone lose a glove?" I yelled down the long corridor, to no response.

Approaching a cluster of people by the elevator, I asked, "Did one of you lose a glove?"

I felt like Prince Charming trying to find the owner of the glass slipper, when, finally, I found my Cinderella. He was sporting thick, dark-brown hair, a shy smile, and a mustache.

"Thanks, that's mine," he said. "My parents just gave me those for my birthday. I can't believe I almost lost it."

"Oh, I'm always losing one glove," I said, doing my best to make Cinderella feel less scatterbrained. "I don't know why they don't just make them in sets of three so you'll always have a spare."

It turned out that Cinderella's name was Adam, and, thanks to a misplaced glove, he would become my very close platonic male friend. In the months and years to come, we shared countless brunches, lunches, dinners, movies. We even had our special place:

04/17/88 POPOVER CAFE	FOOD/BEV	25.08
10/07/90 POPOVER CAFE	FOOD/BEV	31.21
10/13/91 POPOVER CAFE	FOOD/BEV	37.00
04/09/93 POPOVER CAFE	FOOD/BEV	31.00

Now, the trouble with having a male friend you hang out with so much is that any other guy who sees you having dinner, or even Sunday brunch, naturally will assume you're together, and that you are, therefore, off-limits for a pickup.

One Sunday morning, as we were waiting to be seated for brunch at the Popover Café, Adam was taking an exceptionally long time in the men's room when a guy I actually thought I might be interested in started hitting on me. Just as he finished asking for my number, Adam returned. "Oh, I should introduce you guys," I said. "This is John who just moved here from Boston, and this is my cousin, Adam."

From that day on, whenever we were together and met anyone of the opposite sex, we'd introduce each other as Cousin Adam and Cousin Amy.

Then one time we were at a club and I introduced Cousin Adam to a real estate guy from Alabama.

"Great to meet you," he said. "How long have you been dating your cousin?"

My mother never has caught on to the concept of the platonic male friend. Every time I mention that I had dinner with Adam, she always asks, "So where did he take you?"

"He didn't *take* me anywhere," I say. She makes it sound like I'm some portable object, like a CD player or a laptop, that comes with a convenient carrying case.

"Well, he did pay for dinner, right?" she asks.

"No, Mom, why would he pay?" I ask. "He's just a friend."

Eventually, I was able to add, "And anyway, Mom, he has a girlfriend."

"Well, then, drop him like a hot potato," she'd say, "'cause the last thing you need is to put up with a guy who's two-timing."

Returns

I have my own Return Policy: if I happen into a store with a policy that All Sales Are Final, I won't return there. Closet space and money are too scarce.

I remember catching a story on 20/20, or 60 *Minutes*, or one of those other shows with a number in the name, that said fitting rooms are often monitored by same-sex security personnel who can see you from behind what's actually a two-way mirror. As long as the stores are paying the security gals ten bucks an hour to stand back there and look at me, I think it'd be great if they would install a microphone back there, too. That way they could at least offer an opinion and keep me from buying stuff I'll only end up returning. A simple "Thumbs down on the blue dress, sweetie," or "Whoa, that gold tube top looks like maple syrup on a couple of pancakes" could save women like me a whole lot of time, money, and trouble.

Also, if I could only cut down on coffee, I'd be far less likely to make purchasing decisions I end up regretting The Morning After. Of the nearly one hundred returned purchases I counted on my statements, I'm sure a good number were due to severely impaired judgment from shopping on a caffeine high. All it takes is two cups, and, with my endorphins elevated and heart pumping, caffeine goggles make me sure that the fuschia plaid shirt will look just perfect with my lime-green sweater and that my butt looks really shapely in jeans so tight I'll get blood clots.

Then, when the buzz wears off, I'm forced to face the reality that I will probably never wear Santa Claus panties; and, no, it really doesn't make sense to buy something I'll never use—like, say, a vacuum.

Salon Relationships

Any time I question whether I'm even capable of sustaining a long-term relationship, I only need to glance at my Amex statements. They give me hope:

01/14/95 DI TRESSA SALON	HAIR CARE/PRODUCTS	41.20
02/18/95 DI TRESSA SALON	HAIR CARE/PRODUCTS	41.60
03/22/95 DI TRESSA SALON	HAIR CARE/PRODUCTS	67.60
04/22/95 DI TRESSA SALON	HAIR CARE/PRODUCTS	41.60
05/28/95 DI TRESSA SALON	HAIR CARE/PRODUCTS	41.60
06/30/95 DI TRESSA SALON	HAIR CARE/PRODUCTS	57.20
08/27/95 DI TRESSA SALON	HAIR CARE/PRODUCTS	41.60
10/04/95 DI TRESSA SALON	HAIR CARE/PRODUCTS	59.30
11/11/95 DI TRESSA SALON	HAIR CARE/PRODUCTS	41.60
12/10/95 DI TRESSA SALON	HAIR CARE/PRODUCTS	41.60
01/14/96 DI TRESSA SALON	HAIR CARE/PRODUCTS	59.28
02/11/96 DI TRESSA SALON	HAIR CARE/PRODUCTS	41.60
03/17/96 DI TRESSA SALON	HAIR CARE/PRODUCTS	59.28
04/20/96 DI TRESSA SALON	HAIR CARE/PRODUCTS	41.60
05/19/96 DI TRESSA SALON	HAIR CARE/PRODUCTS	41.60
06/22/96 DI TRESSA SALON	HAIR CARE/PRODUCTS	41.60
10/27/96 DI TRESSA SALON	HAIR CARE/PRODUCTS	41.60

11/29/96	DI TRESSA SALON	HAIR CARE/PRODUCTS	59.30
12/27/96	DI TRESSA SALON	HAIR CARE/PRODUCTS	41.60
02/02/97	DI TRESSA SALON	HAIR CARE/PRODUCTS	41.60
03/01/97	DI TRESSA SALON	HAIR CARE/PRODUCTS	59.30
04/11/97	DI TRESSA SALON	HAIR CARE/PRODUCTS	41.60
06/21/97	DI TRESSA SALON	HAIR CARE/PRODUCTS	41.60
07/17/97	DI TRESSA SALON	HAIR CARE/PRODUCTS	41.60
08/23/97	DI TRESSA SALON	HAIR CARE/PRODUCTS	59.28
09/27/97	DI TRESSA SALON	HAIR CARE/PRODUCTS	41.60
11/01/97	DI TRESSA SALON	HAIR CARE/PRODUCTS	41.60
11/29/97	DI TRESSA SALON	HAIR CARE/PRODUCTS	41.60
12/31/97	DI TRESSA SALON	HAIR CARE/PRODUCTS	41.60
02/21/98	DI TRESSA SALON	HAIR CARE/PRODUCTS	41.60
04/10/98	DI TRESSA SALON	HAIR CARE/PRODUCTS	41.60
07/03/98	DI TRESSA SALON	HAIR CARE/PRODUCTS	41.60
08/23/98	DI TRESSA SALON	HAIR CARE/PRODUCTS	41.60
09/26/98	DI TRESSA SALON	HAIR CARE/PRODUCTS	41.60
12/02/98	DI TRESSA SALON	HAIR CARE/PRODUCTS	41.60
12/23/98	DI TRESSA SALON	HAIR CARE/PRODUCTS	41.60
01/16/99	DI TRESSA SALON	HAIR CARE/PRODUCTS	41.60
02/24/99	DI TRESSA SALON	HAIR CARE/PRODUCTS	81.70
03/19/99	DI TRESSA SALON	HAIR CARE/PRODUCTS	41.60
04/13/99	DI TRESSA SALON	HAIR CARE/PRODUCTS	41.60
05/16/99	DI TRESSA SALON	HAIR CARE/PRODUCTS	41.60

I'd been with Rafael for nearly five years. While ending a relationship is never easy, it can be especially hard to wash that man right out of your hair when he happens to be the man who washes your hair, not to mention cuts it, colors it, and blows it dry. It's even tougher to end things with your stylist when he hasn't done anything wrong, but you have an itch for something different. As was the case with Rafael.

Looking back, I don't know why I felt so guilt-ridden for wanting to move on; I'd been totally faithful to Rafael, while the entire time he was clipping and blowing anything with a follicle. Ah, but such is the polygamist nature of Hair Guys.

I think Rafael fancied himself a Doctor of Hair, because he always offered overly technical explanations for things that my gut sensed were not scientifically sound: "You see, in the summer, the hair shaft gets very, *very* thirsty, and if you don't hydrate it vis-à-vis a conditioner, the little bit of natural water-based moisture will automatically seek its own level and be sucked out in the presence of anything fluid-like, be it rain or steam or even orange juice."

I'd humor him with a "Hmm, I never heard that before," rationalizing that it was, in fact, *preferable* that he was no Einstein, since anyone who's ever seen a picture of Al knows he didn't have a clue about hair. And though I'd sometimes fantasize about what miracles another stylist might be able to work on my frizz-prone tresses, the seeds of our split weren't fully planted until one Saturday when, as I strolled home from my dry cleaner, I accidentally met Someone Else. Apparently on a break, the stylist I would come to know as Geri was sipping a cup of coffee in front of a quaint, casement-windowed salon.

"What do you charge for a blow-dry?" I asked, more out of curiosity than genuine interest.

"Twenty-three ninety-five," she answered, unaware of

the seductive powers of a price two dollars less than my current salon, at a location three blocks closer, on a day when I happened to wake looking like the lovechild of Medusa and Buckwheat.

"Can you take me now for a shampoo and blow-dry?" I asked.

"Sure," she said, and beckoned me inside.

Forty minutes later, I left with hair as smooth and silky as Rafael used to make it, but with a slight angle on the sides that was just subtle enough to keep people from exclaiming, "Wow, what did you do to your hair?"

And, just as important, I left with dating advice that only a straight, married woman could be qualified to give.

My one problem now: How to tell Rafael it was over?

Getting *him* to break up with *me* wasn't an option. I don't know anyone who has ever been dumped by their hair guy, and I couldn't imagine what one would have to do to engineer such a thing. Let him find a blob of someone else's conditioner on my collar? Come in smelling like the wrong brand of sculpting gel? I toyed with the notion of having The Talk, but what would I say? "Rafael, we've been together for five years and, uh, I'd . . . I'd . . . I'd like to start seeing other stylists"? And I certainly couldn't ask for my stuff back: "I'm leaving, Rafael, and I'm taking my half a decade's worth of split ends with me . . ."

In the end, I chose the cowardly approach of just fading away, which I reasoned was also the kindest and gentlest way of breaking things off.

What I hadn't planned on, though, was running into him a few months later:

"Amy!" I heard my name shouted from somewhere in the diner. I turned my head from right to left, then left to right, looking for the source of the voice, unknowingly providing my ex-stylist with a 360-degree view of what once was his canvas. My hair, now somewhat shorter, and with a bouncier blow-dry, was obviously being styled by somebody new.

Rafael headed toward my table, smiling. "It's *great* to see you. Your hair looks amazing!" he said, with an exaggerated enthusiasm that was surely a front for his hurt feelings.

Feeling like a well-coiffed cad, I answered, "Thanks," and quickly shifted the conversation away from the sensitive issue of my hair. "And your tan is beautiful," I gushed. "Where'd you get it?"

"Sedona," he said. "You don't even have to try to get a tan there—the sun is just so intense."

"Where'd you stay?" I asked, relieved that, at least for the moment, I'd deftly avoided a direct attack on my fidelity.

"Oh, I guess you didn't know. I moved to Phoenix at the end of June," he said, as nonchalantly as if he were talking about the fact that he'd trimmed his sideburns.

"Why didn't you say anything?" I asked.

"Things were just so crazy before the move—I had to sell pretty much everything and scramble to find a new place—but I figured everyone would find out soon enough, anyway. I didn't expect any of my clients to follow me *that* far."

Everyone would find out soon enough? I had tortured myself with guilt over this guy, and to him I was just part of *everyone*, not even special enough to rate a note or a phone call saying good-bye?

I broke the awkward silence. "Well, it was great seeing you, Rafael, and I wish you luck with everything."

"Thanks," he said, leaning forward as I shifted my cheek for what turned into an air kiss.

You can teach someone to cut hair, I realized, but cutting ties is something you can't learn in beauty school.

Cruising

For the longest time I'd been dying to take a cruise. I wanted to tour palm-tree-covered islands, lounge on the deck with a piña colada, take in cultural events like bingo and shuffle-board.

The problem was finding someone to go with. First I asked Ellie.

"If I were stuck on a ship for a week I'd get claustrophobic," she insisted.

"C'mon," I pleaded, "if you could handle seven years in a four-hundred-square-foot apartment, don't you think you could take seven days on a boat the size of three football fields?"

"Does it include the football players?"

"No."

"Then forget it," she said. "I hear there are hardly any single guys on cruises, and the ones that do go are over seventy."

I asked Sara. "I hear all you do is eat all day," she said, "and then you pig out again at the midnight buffet."

"Well, we'll go to the buffet at 12:01," I suggested, "and you can tell yourself, *I haven't eaten a thing all day.*"

"Nice try," she said, "but I think this year I'm gonna spend a week at a spa."

Then, in a rare moment when my Mom Filter was on the fritz, I mentioned to her that I was considering taking a cruise. But she wasn't any more encouraging: "It'll only make you seasick," she warned. "And if you really want to be nauseous every day, better you should settle down and get pregnant."

Against the advice of practically everyone I knew, I went ahead and put a deposit down to take a seven-night cruise, by myself, to the eastern Caribbean:

02/22/93 CARNIVAL CRUISE RESERVATION	100.00

Three weeks later, I awoke to find myself in a very unsteady universe. The dresser was swaying, the nightstand was swaying, the bed was dipping from side to side.

I was nauseous. I was dizzy.

I was seasick.

My cruise to the eastern Caribbean, however, was not scheduled to leave for another six months. I was at home in my own bed, everything was rocking back and forth, and I was scared.

What was happening?

Slowly, very slowly, I tried to get up, gingerly placing one foot on the floor, then the other. I could feel that the ground below me was firm and solid. This was not an earthquake, I determined.

Could it be stress? I wondered.

Barely a month into my new job at a major New York ad agency, I'd been feeling pressure to prove myself but thought I'd been handling it fairly well. It now took me only two hours to fall asleep instead of my usual three, and my old recurring nightmare of being at a meeting in my panties had scaled back to a onetime dream of showing up at a consumer focus group in my old Brownie uniform.

Yet there I was, dizzier than I'd ever been in my life, with waves of intense nausea cresting in my gut.

I'm not ready to die, I told myself.

And I certainly was not ready to puke on the floor and test the limits of my Stainmaster carpet.

As a trip to the doctor and a five-minute exam would reveal, it wasn't a heart attack, a psychotic break, or anything else that could potentially sentence me to months in bed watching daytime talk shows and soap operas.

"You've just got yourself an inner-ear infection," Dr. Young said calmly, "and as a result you're experiencing vertigo, which is throwing off your whole sense of balance. Get this filled," he said, handing me a prescription, "and it should resolve itself in a couple of weeks."

03/24/93 ANATOLE PHARMACY   **10.00**

The vertigo did resolve itself.

The cynicism about cruising, however, proved to be contagious:

03/31/93 CARNIVAL CRUISE RESERVATION   −100.00 (CREDIT)

but, fortunately, not incurable:

03/22/95 CARNIVAL CRUISE	RESERVATION	879.50
05/23/97 ROYAL CARIBBEAN	CRUISE PAYMENT	1,384.00
02/16/98 CARNIVAL CRUISE	RESERVATION	200.00

The Watch Curse

If you happen to be dating a man who has a birthday coming up, here's my gift suggestion: give him socks, a sweater, or even a boring tie, but if you value this guy at all, whatever you do, do *not* get him a watch.

Apparently, when a man who works in corporate America receives a watch, even from a girlfriend, he automatically thinks it's a retirement gift.

I've given watches as birthday gifts to two different boyfriends—first to Rich the head hunter,

02/12/96 MACY'S	FINE WATCHES	135.31

then to Greg of Wall Street.

01/20/98 SWATCH		108.25

While I was saying, "Happy birthday, honey," and telling him how glad I was to be sharing his special day, he was hearing another speech entirely: *Greg, when you applied to be my boyfriend last March, you came to me with lots of enthusiasm and little experience beyond casual dating and short-term flings. Now, after nearly a year of truly building a mature relationship, I present you with this watch to congratulate you on your progress and to wish you well as you retire from the position of Amy's Guy and move on to bigger and better girlfriends.*

More likely, I think I just jumped the gun on giving such a weighty gift to men who had not yet made up their minds that I was The One. Something so expensive and personal made them think I was way too into the relationship, which must've frightened them enough to run.

What gets me is that they knew *exactly* how fast they were running, too, since the Swiss Army style and the Swatch each had a stopwatch function.

The Cost of Children

It seems like every other year or so the newsmagazines run a cover story on how much money parents will need to raise a child.

So far as I know, nobody has ever published a study about how much you'll have to shell out once your *friends* start having kids.

Here is an informal study of what this single woman has spent on gifts for her married friends' children:

12/17/87	MACY'S	TODDLERS WEAR	31.39
11/26/88	MACY'S	TODDLERS WEAR	16.25
11/26/88	MACY'S	INFANT ACCESSORIES	15.99
05/27/89	LIONEL LEISURE INC	TOYS/CHILDREN ACCESS	19.90
05/11/91	TOYS "R" US	TOYS	43.01
06/11/91	TOYS "R" US	TOYS	21.14
07/30/91	TOYS "R" US	TOYS	25.00
12/14/91	KIDS "R" US	CLOTHES	32.45
04/26/92	BLOOMINGDALE'S	NEWBORN APPAREL	19.49
07/18/93	FAO SCHWARZ	TOY/HOBBY SHOPS	32.48
09/04/93	MACY'S	INFANT ACCESSORIES	16.24
09/09/93	MACY'S	INFANT ACCESSORIES	21.00

The baby announcement is the best investment out there today. For just the cost of a card and a first-class stamp, the rate
of return to the sender, percentage-wise, beats any stock you
could find. Each announcement, including postage, probably
doesn't cost much more than a dollar, with a return of twenty-
dollar terry-cloth sleepers, fifty-dollar Baby Gap gift certifi-
cates, or fifteen-dollar stuffed bunnies. I'm sure Fidelity would
be flooded with investors if they ever decided to start a Baby
Announcement Fund. Believe me, if I could put a dollar in a
mutual fund and get an immediate return of a wool blankie or
a snowsuit or a thirty-dollar Macy's gift card, I'd do it.

09/30/93	GAP KIDS	APPAREL/ACCESSORIES	25.00
12/09/93	TOYS "R" US	TOYS	35.00
12/10/93	TOYS "R" US	TOYS	43.28
01/22/94	MACY'S	TOYS	32.48
04/02/94	TOYS "R" US	TOYS	10.80
05/21/94	TOYS "R" US	TOYS	10.81
07/07/94	MACY'S	NEWBORN CLOTHING	22.00
10/23/94	MACY'S	NEWBORN CLOTHING	39.00
11/23/94	TOYS "R" US	TOYS	10.81
02/03/95	BLOOMINGDALE'S	INFANT LAYETTE	36.26
03/11/95	BLOOMINGDALE'S	GIRLS 2-14 FURNISHINGS	15.16
03/12/95	FAO SCHWARZ	TOYS/HOBBIES/GAMES	204.60
04/14/95	TOYS "R" US	TOYS	17.62
04/15/95	GAP KIDS	APPAREL/ACCESSORIES	18.40
05/10/95	FAO SCHWARZ	TOYS/HOBBIES/GAMES	5.41

Please understand, though, that I'm not regretting one
penny of what I've spent to welcome a close friend's or rela-

tive's Little Angel to the world. Kids tend to remember you
by the gifts you give, and it's actually nice when the child
gets to be four or five and knows you as Mommy's Friend
Who Gave You the Stuffed Hippo. (It's rare that you'll hear,
"This is Mommy's Friend Who Gave You the Forty-Dollar
Gift Card," but the parents appreciate it, so I still give them,
anyway.) Bringing a life into the world is such a huge
achievement, such a joyous moment, that it certainly should
be recognized by friends and family.

05/10/95	FAO SCHWARZ	TOYS/HOBBIES/GAMES	15.70
09/03/95	FAO SCHWARZ	TOYS/HOBBIES/GAMES	14.06
09/16/95	FAO SCHWARZ	TOY/HOBBY SHOPS	122.31
12/16/95	FAO SCHWARZ CATALOG	TOY/HOBBY SHOPS	76.25
09/11/96	MACY'S	12-24 MONTHS	19.70
09/11/96	TOYS "R" US	TOYS	16.23
12/21/96	TOYS "R" US	TOYS	50.00

What I resent is the friends I haven't spoken to in years—
some of whom never return my phone calls—who send out
announcements that seem to be official requests for gifts.
One such friend had the nerve to send a mass email before
the baby was born: "Just wanted to give everyone the heads-
up that we'll be doing the baby's room in light blue, a subtle
hint to those of you wondering what color crib sheets to
buy!"

| 12/21/96 | TOYS "R" US | TOYS | 22.65 |
| 06/25/97 | FAO SCHWARZ | TOYS/HOBBIES/GAMES | 34.64 |

07/06/97	TOYS "R" US	TOYS	64.94
09/01/97	TOYS "R" US	TOYS	19.01
09/21/97	MACY'S	LAYETTE, 0-9 MONTHS	39.42
09/21/97	TOYS "R" US	TOYS	14.26
12/23/97	GAP KIDS	APPAREL/ACCESSORIES	50.00

The traditional information people give out in baby announcements has also always bothered me—why the obsession with height and weight? Just think how inappropriate it'd be if we included similar stats in wedding announcements: *Mr. and Mrs. Irving Glickwater are pleased to announce the marriage of their daughter Pamela, five foot two and 167 lbs., to David Harrison, five-ten, 240 lbs., and, optimistically, on Atkins.*

Okay, well, since I know it's only a matter of time before all my friends' kids grow up and need graduation gifts, I'm going to give Fidelity a call so I can start a college fund.

(In)Security

Being single with your own apartment means you can listen to music as loud as you want it, have a lime-green couch with a fuschia throw rug, and wake up as early as you want without having to tiptoe around for fear of disturbing a husband or roommate.

As my mother was astute enough to point out, it also means that you could keel over and have rigor mortis set in before anyone even realizes it's been three weeks since you left your apartment.

I came home from work one night to find her cheery message blaring over the machine:

"Amila? I just realized that I don't even have a set of keys to your apartment. I know I asked you for one about a year ago, and you never made me a set. What if something happened and you were laying there and nobody could get into your apartment? Even if I flew up there, you'd end up laying there until I could locate a locksmith, then you'd lay a little longer until the locksmith would come over, and you would just lay and lay . . ."

When my mother, who moonlights as Chief of the Grammar Police, totally violates the rules of "lie" versus "lay,"

I know she's speaking from her heart. However, whether I'd in fact be laying or lying, I'd definitely be lying to say that, in the far recesses of my mind, I didn't share her concern. She continued her die-atribe: "By the time we got in, even if you were totally coherent, you'd be so stiff from laying there, they'd have to administer fifty cc's of Ben Gay."

Suddenly I remembered Jordan, the twenty-eight-year-old account executive from a former ad-agency job who, though apparently healthy, had had an aneurism at his desk and was found dead by the cleaning lady. What if it had happened at home and nobody had the keys to get in? Who would have found him then?

I deluded myself into thinking I had solved the problem when I decided to make spare sets of keys for my friends Sara and Ellie, both of whom live less than five minutes away.

02/20/98 EAST TOP LOCK   LOCKS/KEYS   5.46

But then, just as I was about to lull myself into a false sense of security, I had to ask myself: What would happen if I couldn't get to the phone and nobody even *knew* I needed help? Alll the spare sets of keys in the world wouldn't help if I were lying on the floor without a telephone.

It was then that I remembered the words of a woman whose voice resounded through my brain almost as clearly as my mother's: "HELP!!!!! I'VE FALLEN AND I CAN'T GET UP!!!!!"

On February 24, 1998, I became, I suspect, the youngest, healthiest person ever to attempt to enlist the services of the

Life Alert corporation, the company famous for their quirky commercials about the old lady who fell in her living room.

My call was answered by a friendly woman with a Southern accent who immediately asked for my zip code.

"One-oh-oh-one-seven," I told her.

"We certainly service Manhattan," she confirmed.

New York must be a gold mine for Life Alert, I thought. We don't just have people who've *fallen* and can't get up—we have people who were intentionally *pushed.*

After receiving a brochure in the mail, I decided that maybe I could wait a few years before signing up. Like single people everywhere, I would try my best to live with the risk that I might have to lie there. And then I'd lie a little longer. And then I'd just lie and lie and lie . . .

TGIM

I'd often thought it but had never had the balls to say it: TGIM.

Yup, Thank God It's Monday.

I knew it was blasphemy, since anyone under thirty-five is supposed to live for the weekends and the big Saturday-night date, but, the truth is, there are times when life on your own is so quiet that you actually *miss* the office—you look forward to gossiping with your work friends, stopping at the coffee machine to discuss the latest episode of *Desperate Housewives*. Sometimes, saying "Good morning" to the receptionist may seem as close as you can get to the warmth of a "Honey, I'm home."

Then again, no matter how much you miss your work buddies, when the only human contact of your weekend was saying "not interested" to a telemarketer, you dread the Monday Morning Question. "So," it usually begins, posed by a smiley, perky, married coworker who's just dying to tell you about a picnic in the park or some other coupley thing she did with her man, "what did you do this weekend?"

Even my mother pressures me about the weekends.

(Beep.) "Hi, Amila. It's Saturday night at nine-thirty. I guess you're vacuuming and didn't hear the phone. Anyway, honey, I would suggest you put down the vacuum and see if you can find a singles dance. 'Cause how are you gonna feel when one day your friends all want you to meet their new husbands and you're sitting there, saying, 'I'd like to introduce you to my clean rug'?"

So what *do* I do on the weekends? An analysis of my American Express statements from 1987 through 1999 shows that what I did nearly every Saturday and Sunday was eat (mostly takeout), shop, and run errands.

I'd like to think I had *some* exciting Saturday nights that aren't on my charge bills because somebody else picked up the tab. Though I do feel that women in our culture put way too much importance on the Saturday-night date. I'm sure that right now, somewhere in America, a couple of women are having a conversation pretty much like this:

Woman 1: So David took me to the Rainbow Room for dinner, gave me three dozen red roses, and asked me to marry him.
Woman 2: What night was it?
Woman 1: Thursday.
Woman 2: He's not into you. Move on.

My Career as a
Country Singer

Though I'm a huge fan of Ringling Brothers and Barnum & Bailey, my escape fantasies never included running away to join the circus, because every year at least three different circuses come to my neighborhood, and true escape fantasies should embrace possibilities completely out of the realm of one's everyday life. No, my major fantasy, being a career woman from New York, is to move to Nashville and become a country singer.

It all started with the purchase of a Dolly Parton CD, an impulse buy for myself while I was shopping for a Barbra Streisand cassette for my mother's birthday:

```
12/10/97  TOWER RECORDS        MUSIC/ACCESSORIES   36.96
```

Then, about a month later, I found something that could help me *be* Dolly Parton. Yep, I moseyed on over to my local drugstore an' picked me up one of them Country Classics karaoke CDs:

```
01/05/98  DUANE READE                              7.14
```

I was well aware that I didn't have the required background for a career in country music. I didn't get married at sixteen; it was hard enough to even find a boyfriend by thirty-five. I wasn't broke; it was just my lack of time and organizational skills that kept me from paying my bills by the due dates. And my "man" wasn't cheating on me; Danny was only a platonic friend, so why shouldn't he date?

I did think that, just maybe, I could break new ground with the professional woman's country album, with songs like "Hey, Good Lookin', What Ya Got from the Takeout Place?"; or "If I Told You You Had a Beautiful Body, Would You File a Harassment Suit?"; or maybe "You Were Always on My PalmPilot"?

Far-fetched as it may have been, I thought I had enough music in my genes to make this just a hair more realistic than a pipe dream. My father has been playing the drums since he was sixteen, and my mother was one of the top violinists in her high school. Vocally, we have quite a history as well. I'll never forget the day when I heard my mother sing in the Broadway production of *Forty-second Street*. She was in the third row of the mezzanine, and after the fifth person shushed her, I wanted to slide under my seat and disappear. My big sister, Judy, also had a moment as a public songstress when, at age ten, she belted out "Hello, Dolly!" in the Little Miss America pageant; the judges voted her into the semifinals, but she passed out from the gnat-filled humid air of New Jersey's Palisades Amusement Park and missed her chance to sing in the next round.

* * *

When I booked my four-day trip to Nashville,

```
04/06/98 DELTA AIRLINES      PASSENGER TICKET   202.00
```

I was especially excited about seeing all the top-name country acts at the Grand Ole Opry.

```
04/04/98 OPRYLAND PARK CTR, NASHVILLE TN          19.49
```

I'd also heard that there were bars near Nashville's music row where amateurs like myself could belt one out in front of a real audience. I relished my chance to be the first Borkowsky to sing country music and, more important, the first Borkowsky to sing publicly, uninterrupted by gnats or irate theatergoers.

Ah, but it was not to be. Two days before my "gig" at the Grand Ole Opry, I got lassoed up and roped into doing a super-rush ad campaign for a new soft drink, and had to work the weekend.

```
04/09/98 OPRYLAND PARK CTR, NASHVILLE TN -19.49(CREDIT)
```

I put my country-singing dreams on the shelf, not knowing if I'd ever get to Nashville, and, as if that weren't bad enough, I lost nearly $200 on a nonrefundable airline ticket.

If only I'd had a dog who died that same weekend, I could have written a country song about it.

The Tarot of Leg Hair

07/19/94 CAESARS ATLANTIC CITY   BUFFET   8.99

I took a bus trip with a couple of girlfriends to Atlantic City, an excursion on which the only highlight was getting our fortunes told by a totally off-base palm reader. Not only did the auburn-haired stranger and the trip to Asia she predicted never materialize, she didn't even get my *present* right, claiming that I was torn between two guys when in fact I hadn't had a date in five months.

If they really want to know what's going on with a woman, I think that fortune tellers should forget about reading palms and start reading legs. Here's a list of guidelines the Madame Rosas of the world could use to more accurately assess any woman's situation:

> *Hair growth on legs of a quarter- to a half-inch = not dating anyone.*
>
> *Hair growth greater than half an inch = will take trip in near future, to waxing salon.*
>
> *Smooth, hairless legs = dating someone or has doctor's appointment.*

*Slight stubble (eighth-inch or less) = has boyfriend
    but he's out of town.*

*One leg smooth and other stubbly = working crazy
    hours, ran out of shaving gel.*

*Both legs shaved from knees down only = had blind
    date from computer, wore pants.*

*Hairless legs with cuts = rushed through shave for
    booty call.*

The Miracles of Caller ID

06/06/94 RADIO SHACK   30.25

There was a time when a newfangled device known as caller ID allowed mere mortals like myself to astound less savvy people with what appeared to be uncanny psychic abilities.

Of course, the real reason caller ID was created was to give us more control over who we talked to and when. As such, it's the perfect device for fully functioning adults like myself who, though we love our mothers and wouldn't trade them for all the latte in Starbucks, sometimes just aren't in the mood to be reminded that we'd better floss daily because Phyllis Mellstein's daughter had gums that blew up like a balloon and now she needs upper *and* lower dentures and she's only twenty-eight.

Plus, it doesn't hurt that caller ID keeps me from picking up the phone when some great guy I just met calls, and I don't want him to know that I'm illegally parked on the couch on a Saturday night.

Suddenly, a little plastic box with an LCD display became the bouncer for my own private Studio 54, letting me pick and choose who got beyond my velvet rope.

Now, as someone who's spent many a night with a silent phone, there are times I appreciate that anyone calls me at all. So, along with the exhilaration, I felt an undercurrent of intense guilt as I contemplated my life with the new little box as my gatekeeper.

"The thing is not to let anyone know you have it," advised the Radio Shack guy. "Once they know you have caller ID, if you don't pick up, they're going to think you're avoiding them." He was right: as long as I didn't *tell* anyone about my new purchase, potential boyfriends, ex-boyfriends, girlfriends I could only take in small doses, and, most of all, my mother, would never have to suffer knowing they didn't make the cut.

About ten minutes after I hooked up the box, my phone rang, and I rushed to the kitchen counter to see whether it was someone I wanted to talk to. I glanced at the display window, hoping the number would be one I'd recognize (it would be years before caller ID was capable of showing the corresponding name).

Instead of a number, all I saw was a series of letters that spelled out the two most disappointing words: "Unknown Caller."

I was now getting concerned about possibly missing an urgent call. What if it was my mother, I worried, and there was a family emergency? Or, worse yet, what if she had critical news to tell me about a surge in the pollen count or a recall on my brand of panty liners?

Though if it were really so important, I reasoned, she'd leave a message when my machine picked up.

As it turned out, my first caller ID box showed nearly

everyone who rang my line as an Unknown Caller. Twenty-nine calls later, as I scrolled through my thirty-call-capacity caller ID box, I saw that the only people who hadn't shown up as Unknown Callers were my friends Ellie and Adam.

A few years later, when phones started coming with a built-in caller ID display, I bought a new phone and tried the service again:

12/14/99 RADIO SHACK   **54.30**

It had improved to where most numbers, including Mom's, were clearly displayed on the screen. However, it wasn't long before some news show ran a story on how to outsmart caller ID, and my mother got cagey and started using call blocking. Now whenever my phone says "Unknown Caller," I know there's an excellent chance that it's my mother.

I'm sure she was happy to have found a way to protect her identity, and, I confess, I was even happier. Now that she showed up again as Unknown Caller, I was relieved of any guilt at screening her calls.

After all, wasn't it my mother who, since I was two, told me not to talk to people I didn't know?

Maintenance

A loaded gun and me, alone in my apartment on a Saturday night, is a very dangerous combination.

Especially when that gun is a caulking gun . . .

. . . and I've had absolutely no training or experience in handling it.

My gun came preloaded with almond-colored latex caulking, and though I would've preferred to need latex in the bedroom that night instead of in the bath, a quiet evening at home seemed the perfect time to try to mend the growing gap between my bathtub and the wall. For nearly a year I'd been meaning to redo the corroded caulking, but with so many projects on my list, from cleaning closets to putting up bookshelves, I'd been starting to think that I might never tackle it.

I thought back to the time my friend Cindy showed me what she was giving her husband for Valentine's Day: a circular metal disc engraved with the words "To It."

"What's that?" I asked.

"If you were married you'd get it," she said.

"C'mon, clue me in," I pressed.

"Well, whenever I ask Rich to do something around the house—like fixing the faucet or cleaning out the garage or whatever—he always says, 'I'll do it when I get around to it.' So I'm giving him a round To-It."

Yeah, it was cutesy, but by deciding to go on a caulking rampage that night, I had essentially given myself my own round To-It, a realization that made me feel as self-sufficient as it did pathetic.

According to the directions on the tube, to begin, all I had to do was snip the tip with some scissors.

Basically, I would be performing a circumcision, an area in which I have even less experience than home repair.

After several fruitless attempts at tip-snipping—my plastic-handled scissors were unable to make even a faint dent in the plastic—I took the tube into the kitchen and set it down on the cutting board. With one swift stroke of the carving knife the tip flew off, and a remarkably even length of rich, creamy caulking squirted out.

Then, just as I was about to test-pull the trigger, the phone rang.

I glanced at my new-and-improved caller ID and saw that it wasn't my mother or a guy I was interested in. So I picked up.

"How ya dooooooooooooooin?" came the voice from Chattanooga. It was Randy, my Southern-fried friend, a married suburban homeowner with two kids who is a genuine

Mr. Fixit. At least, he always sounds like he knows what he's doing. I haven't actually seen him in ten years, so for all I know, he could live in two thousand square feet of peeling plaster, jammed garage doors, and toilets that are missing their rubber gaskets.

"What're ya doin' home on a Saturday night?" he asked, with that expectant tone married friends often have when they're hoping for the vicarious thrill of having called at the *wrong time*.

"Just making my way to the bathroom with my caulking gun," I told him.

"Oh, wanna talk later, then?"

"No, now's good," I replied, confident that I could caulk and talk at the same time. "Actually, I could use your help. Once I squeeze the gunk out, what do I use to smooth it down?"

"Just go ahead and smooth it down with your finger."

"A finger," I repeated. "I think I have one of those in my toolbox."

I let my fingers do the caulking as Randy regaled me with stories of family life, heartwarming tales of refereeing fights, cutting bubble gum out of hair, and spending New Year's Eve with a feverish two-year-old in the emergency room. Finally he was summoned away for the important mission of scraping baby poop off a piano bench. I toughed it out in the bathroom for another twenty minutes until I was sure every millimeter of gap was filled up with caulk.

I felt accomplished and empowered, happy to be living my life of freedom, proud that I was not just my own woman, I was My Own Handyman.

I stood back to admire my handiwork, to observe for the first time the gestalt of my newly repaired tub.

Apparently, while I was crouched down with my caulking gun, some six-year-old had slipped in and glopped Silly Putty all around my bathtub.

How could I not have seen that I'd gotten trigger-happy? That my entire tub was surrounded by a line thick enough to run down the middle of a highway?

I called Randy back. "It seemed fine while I was doing it," I told him, "but when I stepped back to look, all I could see was this fat line of beige gunk."

"The color changes when it dries," he informed me. "Trust me. Just forget about it, and it'll look a lot better in the morning."

Figuring that if I stood back even farther, I'd have that much more perspective, I repositioned myself several blocks uptown and met my friend Danny for some late-night salmon teriyaki:

12/04/95 TOTOYA	37.30

I told myself that, if I had to, I could peel the caulking off and just start over. When I got a round To-It.

A New Routine?

02/26/97 AMERICA WEST AIRLINES

AIR TRANSPORTATION   −549.00 (CREDIT)

I don't remember where I first heard of Sedona, Arizona, but for almost as far back as I could remember, I'd wanted to take a trip there to see its legendary cloudless blue skies, enjoy the non-frizzing dry weather, and experience a sense of tranquillity that would be a welcome break from the nutty pace of Manhattan. After booking my flight, I called the Sedona Chamber of Commerce. They were kind enough to send me a brochure of the available tours, which convinced me that, gorgeous as it may be, Sedona did not offer quite enough variety for my taste.

Tour A invited me to view "magnificent panoramas of red rocks."

Tour B promised "awe-inspiring formations of red rocks."

Tour C "explores the geologic marvels of red rocks."

Or, for a change of pace, Tour D would provide a "once-in-a-lifetime red rock experience."

The offerings went all the way through the grand tour, Tour H, which, as I recall, went pretty much like this: "The day begins as you climb aboard our red rock motorcoach to explore the heart of red rock country, where you can see everything from red rock vistas to historic red rock carvings and, *if time allows*, dramatic cliffs of red rocks. The tour includes an opportunity to photograph red rocks, study red rocks, and climb red rocks, and those who choose the optional extension can enjoy dinner at a local eatery constructed entirely of red rocks. The tour concludes with red rocks and more red rocks and so many red rocks that you'll have red rocks coming out of your nostrils and pouring out of your ears and you'll be up to your ass in red rocks and all you'll see, think about, or speak about is red red red rocks rocks rocks red rocks red rocks red rocks red rocks red rocks and red red red rocks rocks rocks red rocks red rocks red rocks red rocks red rocks and red red red rocks rocks rocks red rocks red rocks red rocks red rocks red rocks and red red red rocks rocks rocks red rocks red rocks red rocks red rocks.

My whole purpose in going away was to have a change in my routine, not to trade it for an even more repetitive one. I know lots of people rave about Sedona—the relaxing climate, the clear blue skies, and, yes, the majestic red rocks. However, for someone like me, who is seeking variety, nightlife, and single guys, to travel alone to Sedona, I'd need to have rocks in my head—and somehow I just know what color they'd be.

My Favorite Things

On the rare occasion that anyone asks me, "Where's your favorite place to shop?" I answer with total candor that I don't have one. If a store happens to have an item I want or need at a price that's not outrageous, I'll buy it—but, no, I don't have a favorite store.

Twelve years of Amex bills, however, tell a different story:

12/17/87	MACY'S	ESTEE LAUDER COSMETICS	16.24
01/02/88	MACY'S	CONTEMPORARY COATS	97.41
07/31/88	MACY'S	GIFT BONDS	25.00
12/15/88	MACY'S	MISSES FRAGRANCES	32.48
02/05/89	MACY'S	JR JEANS	32.46
07/12/89	MACY'S	CONTEMPORARY DAYWEAR	23.80
07/16/89	MACY'S	DESIGNER SWIMWEAR	53.03
08/04/89	MACY'S	TRADITIONAL SHOES	68.19
08/11/89	MACY'S	DAY/MODERATE DRESSES	91.01
09/22/89	MACY'S	MODERATE TRADITIONAL SHOES	104.90
10/04/89	MACY'S	TRADITIONAL SHOES	50.01
11/20/89	MACY'S	DAY/MODERATE DRESSES	68.99

12/30/89	MACY'S	JR SEPARATES	77.84
01/14/90	MACY'S	14KT GOLD COLLECTIONS	48.71
03/31/90	MACY'S	YOUNG JR DRESSES	32.46
06/16/90	MACY'S	MACY'S ATHLETIC CLUB	39.78
08/18/90	MACY'S	VACUUM CLEANERS	108.24
08/19/90	MACY'S	VACUUM CLEANERS	−108.24 (CREDIT)
09/05/90	MACY'S	ESTEE LAUDER	17.86
10/04/90	MACY'S	TRADITIONAL SHOES	57.37
12/16/90	MACY'S	MISSES FRAGRANCES	37.89
01/26/91	MACY'S	CLUBHOUSE KNITWEAR	51.96
02/15/91	MACY'S	PILLOWS	70.33
04/28/91	MACY'S	GROCERY ITEMS	9.95
06/16/91	MACY'S	JR KNITS	25.98
11/02/91	MACY'S	MODERATE TRADITIONAL SHOES	124.48
12/11/91	MACY'S	BOYS WEAR (SIZES 4-7)	31.39
12/27/91	MACY'S	ELECTRIC RAZORS	42.22
02/17/92	MACY'S	DESIGNER COSMETICS	19.49
05/03/92	MACY'S	DENIM AND WOVENS	31.39
06/28/92	MACY'S	SEPARATES AND SWEATERS	75.22
07/11/92	MACY'S	SEPARATES AND SWEATERS	21.64
07/25/92	MACY'S	HOUSEWARE GIFTS	32.48
08/02/92	MACY'S	NY SOCIAL OCCASN JR DRS	102.62
12/17/92	MACY'S	JR COLLECTIONS	24.35
02/20/93	MACY'S	DAY/MODERATE DRESSES	−80.11 (CREDIT)
04/12/93	MACY'S	ESTEE LAUDER	18.94
05/23/93	MACY'S	LUGGAGE	189.44
07/15/93	MACY'S	HANDBAGS	59.54
09/04/93	MACY'S	FASHION WATCHES	21.65
09/05/93	MACY'S	DRESSES	64.94

10/02/93	MACY'S	JEWELRY	25.98
11/28/93	MACY'S	HOUSEWARE GIFTS	40.05
12/09/93	MACY'S	COSTUME JEWELRY	24.36
12/09/93	MACY'S	ROBES	43.29
12/10/93	MACY'S	PEARLS	6.48
12/10/93	MACY'S	JR KNITS	28.12
01/22/94	MACY'S	TOYS	32.48
04/30/94	MACY'S	FRAGRANCES	51.96
07/04/94	MACY'S	GIFT CERTIFICATE	50.00
09/24/94	MACY'S	HANDBAGS	27.06
10/23/94	MACY'S	FASHION HOSIERY	36.26
11/23/94	MACY'S	JEWELRY	97.43
12/03/94	MACY'S	STATIONERY/DESK ACC	32.45
12/10/94	MACY'S	GIFT CERTIFICATE	100.00
01/22/95	MACY'S	FASHION HOSIERY	11.37
02/05/95	MACY'S	KNITS	39.35
03/23/95	MACY'S	CAREER DRESSES	21.64
06/04/95	MACY'S	ALL OTHER DENIM	18.39
06/04/95	MACY'S	PL PEARLS/SOCIAL	8.66
01/13/96	MACY'S	ESTEE LAUDER COSMETICS	20.03
02/12/96	MACY'S	FINE WATCHES	135.31
06/15/96	MACY'S	CARDS & WRAP NON-ITEM	2.11
06/21/96	MACY'S	LUGGAGE	86.59
09/11/96	MACY'S	PERSONAL ELECTRICS	10.79
12/21/96	MACY'S	WOVEN TOPS	48.70
06/28/97	MACY'S	BETTER RELATED SEPARATES	21.65
09/27/97	MACY'S	MOD SMALL LEATHER GOOD,	
		YOUNG ATTITUDES	86.59
11/22/97	MACY'S	MOD SMALL LEATHER GOOD	
			−32.46 (CREDIT)

02/20/98 MACY'S	LUGGAGE	75.76
04/19/98 MACY'S	RAINWEAR	−20.30 (CREDIT)
05/12/98 MACY'S	TOWELS	42.39
07/16/98 MACY'S	PILLOWS	71.90
09/27/98 MACY'S	YOUNG ATTITUDES RAINWEAR	75.78
11/07/98 MACY'S	RESTAURANT	11.64
11/07/98 MACY'S	SWEATERS, CAREER DRESSES	218.65
12/24/98 MACY'S	BRAS	3.78
01/23/99 MACY'S	PANTIES	15.00
03/21/99 MACY'S	HAIR GOODS	11.37
04/17/99 MACY'S	CASUAL SLEEPWEAR	27.60
04/17/99 MACY'S	GIFT WRAP	5.95
04/24/99 MACY'S	PANTIES	5.41
04/24/99 MACY'S	SOCKS	7.04
07/14/99 MACY'S	BRAS/PANTIES/SHAPEWEAR	48.17
08/20/99 MACY'S	WOMEN'S SIZE SLEEPWEAR	21.22
12/18/99 MACY'S	MOD CAS PETITE SPTWEAR	42.88

Snoopy and Garfield never spent a dime at Macy's, yet every Thanksgiving they get their own floats in the big parade. If Macy's were smart, they'd recognize and reward my loyalty by allowing me to ride in their next parade, as Macy's Best Customer. Decked out in my Traditional Shoes and Contemporary Daywear, I'd stand proudly on my float, smiling as I waved my Fashion Watch–clad wrist. And if the Macy's folks don't think this would be jazzy enough to be parade-worthy, I could turn it up a notch and shave my legs *live* with my razor from Personal Electrics, and apply my Estée Lauder Foundation in front of *millions* of spectators, all the while wearing Designer Swimwear—a living, breathing reminder that along with the blessings of family and health and wealth, this Thanksgiving we should all be grateful for Denim and Wovens, Houseware Gifts, and Fashion Hosiery, all at moderate prices—and *less* if you have a coupon!

Insomnia

My name is Amy, and I'm an insomniac.

Thinking peace and quiet might help, I bought wax earplugs.

08/07/87 PLAZA EASTSIDE DRUGS		
	PRESCRIPTIONS/SUNDRIES	3.79

They melted in my ears, and I had to go to the emergency room to have them surgically removed.

I bought foam earplugs.

01/18/89 DUANE READE	PRESCRIPTIONS/SUNDRIES	3.11

Luckily, they didn't melt, but they wouldn't stay in my ears at all because the foam was so springy.

Focus on the basics, I told myself, and I bought a nice, new, firm mattress,

02/26/91 DIAL-A-MATTRESS	BEDDING	324.11

which gave my back excellent support while I lay there awake.

I got myself a padded sleeping mask.

08/05/95 NOUVEL LUGGAGE	ACCESSORIES	8.66

It was one hundred percent effective at making me look like the Lone Ranger.

I felt I'd exhausted every possible solution and, most of all, myself.

I would lie in bed worrying about deadlines at work, smile lines on my face, long lines at the post office that would keep me from sending my taxes in on time. I'd lose sleep over the fact that I was losing sleep.

Then one day I happened across an article on America Online that I hoped would change my life. It said that turkey and bananas contain the sleep-inducing chemical tryptophan. Suddenly, "Can you please send over a hot open-faced turkey sandwich and a banana?" became my mantra.

02/27/96 TIVOLI	FOOD AND BEVERAGE	15.00
02/28/96 TIVOLI	FOOD AND BEVERAGE	13.78
03/03/96 TIVOLI	FOOD AND BEVERAGE	15.00
03/06/96 TIVOLI	FOOD AND BEVERAGE	15.20
03/10/96 TIVOLI	FOOD AND BEVERAGE	14.75

I'm sorry to have to report that weeks of Turkey-and-Banana Therapy did not help me sleep at all and a couple of times even backfired. I'd doze off on the couch, watching *Court TV*, only to be awakened by the doorman buzzing my intercom: "Amy, it's Shabbir. Your food is here."

I have, therefore, come to the following conclusions about the sleep-inducing effects of turkey and bananas. I sincerely hope my findings will keep you from throwing out unnecessary money on your own research.

Turkey is an effective sleep aid only when served at large family gatherings that include uncles who repeat the same stories over and over, many bottles of wine, and well-meaning third cousins with whom you have nothing in common but a bloodline.

Bananas are *never* effective at making you sleepy. Just think about who on our planet eats the most bananas. It's monkeys, of course, and monkeys are the most wired, *hyperactive* creatures you'll ever find. I've seen monkeys swing from vines, scratch their heads, groom their hair, and groom their friends' hair, but one thing I've never seen a monkey do is *sleep*.

After years of trial and error, I found the one thing, the only thing, that truly helps me fall asleep: reading in bed.

05/05/99 BORDERS BOOKS	BOOKS/SUPPLIES/GIFTS	88.91
07/18/99 BARNES & NOBLE	BOOKS	22.35
07/23/99 BORDERS BOOKS	BOOKS/SUPPLIES/GIFTS	8.11

I don't know if it's because reading gives me something to focus on other than my own worries, or because the eyestrain from focusing on the type makes me sleepy, or because the—*Hello? Hello? Okay, I guess you dozed off. Pleasant dreams.*

The Necessity of Makeup

My mother has always been proud to claim that I have her eyes, and my father has always held firm to his belief that I have his nose.

The truth is, I got my face from a woman named Estée:

12/17/87 MACY'S	ESTEE LAUDER COSMETICS	16.24
06/03/89 ABRAHAM & STRAUS	ESTEE LAUDER COSMETICS	17.32
01/21/90 BLOOMINGDALE'S	ESTEE LAUDER COSMETICS	17.86
09/05/90 MACY'S	ESTEE LAUDER COSMETICS	17.86
05/26/91 BERGDORF GOODMAN	ESTEE LAUDER COSMETICS	31.93
09/28/91 BLOOMINGDALE'S	ESTEE LAUDER COSMETICS	17.86
01/21/92 MACY'S	ESTEE LAUDER COSMETICS	18.94

We're related not by blood but by octylmethoxycinnamate and titanium dioxide. Yet to Estée's credit, this doesn't seem to make any difference, and she gives me gifts as if I were her own daughter. Through the years, she's given me *Free With Purchase!* eleven zippered makeup cases, nineteen lipsticks, half a dozen tiny jars of eye cream, and countless other thoughtful and age-defying gifts. As with most presents, they're not necessarily all things I can use. Though a free gift is a terrible thing to waste, recently I had to throw away two little bottles of night cream from the eighties because a circle of glop and crust had formed around the cap. It's a sad day when you notice that products designed to prevent visible signs of aging have visibly aged.

01/26/92	BLOOMINGDALE'S	ESTEE LAUDER COSMETICS	18.94
05/02/92	BLOOMINGDALE'S	ESTEE LAUDER COSMETICS	18.94
05/04/92	BLOOMINGDALE'S	ESTEE LAUDER COSMETICS	37.89
04/12/93	MACY'S	ESTEE LAUDER COSMETICS	18.94
08/15/93	BLOOMINGDALE'S	ESTEE LAUDER COSMETICS	13.53
08/21/93	MACY'S	ESTEE LAUDER COSMETICS	18.94
09/06/94	BLOOMINGDALE'S	ESTEE LAUDER COSMETICS	20.03
02/04/95	BLOOMINGDALE'S	ESTEE LAUDER COSMETICS	20.03

But Estée must be doing something right, because at one point Rick, a guy I'd been sort-of-kind-of-but-not-really-dating, said what all guys eventually say to me: "Amy, why do you always have to wear makeup? You don't need it. Why don't you go without makeup, just for a day?"

"Okay," I agreed. I was afraid of being Lauder-less, but I was also in my smooth-skinned twenties and bravely willing to give it a go.

The next day, there was the question: "Are you okay?"

"Why?" I said.

Rick studied my face again and answered: "You look like you're about to pass out."

Then there was the time I found Matthew, a sculptor I'd been dating for over a year, in my bathroom dabbing my Estée

Lauder Fresh Air Makeup Base on his face, engaging in the cosmetics equivalent of cross-dressing.

"What are you doing?" I asked.

"Just trying to hide a zit," he answered, as he continued happily Laudering his forehead.

"What zit?" I asked. "Your face looks fine."

"That's 'cause I put your makeup on it," he answered.

A short time later, Matthew and I faded, faded to where even the deepest shade of honey-bronze foundation couldn't help us.

But Estée and I, well, that's a different story:

05/27/95 MACY'S	ESTEE LAUDER COSMETICS	20.02
01/13/96 MACY'S	ESTEE LAUDER COSMETICS	20.03
06/22/96 MACY'S	ESTEE LAUDER COSMETICS	20.03
11/29/96 STERNS	ESTEE LAUDER COSMETICS	20.03
09/27/97 MACY'S	ESTEE LAUDER COSMETICS	29.77

The World's Best Allergist

I liked Dr. B. instantly. A white-haired, gentle, grandpa type who appeared to be nearing eighty, he wisely kept my expectations low. "Vee vill start you on zee shots," he said, in an accent that made him sound more like a Freudian shrink than an allergist, "and maybe in a few months you vill see a leetle less sneezing and, hopefully, vee vill control zee runny nose a leetle bit, too." I wasn't sure that cabbing it across town every week for something that *maybe* would make my allergies a "leetle" better would be worth the effort, but with a doctor who made shots seem anything but scary, I was willing to try:

08/04/93 ALLERGY/IMMUN	COPAY	10.00

Each week, Dr. B. would remind me to "vait in the vaiting room" to make sure I didn't have a reaction to the serum. "Gif it thirty minutes 'cause vee vant to make sure you're tolerating the shot vell." When a half-hour had passed, he would return to the waiting room, check that the injection site wasn't swollen, and send me on my way with a paternal pat on the arm and an approving "Looks goot!"

Dr. B. turned out to be a magician with a syringe for a wand. Amazingly, just five "looks goots" later—barely over a month from my first shot—my sneezing was cut in half, my nose had completely stopped running, and I could finally use my tissues the way they were meant to be used: as emergency toilet paper in dive bars.

Three years later, Dr. B. announced that he was retiring and closing his practice. That Thursday, I left his office with a runny nose and red, watery eyes, none of which had anything to do with allergies.

Chinese Mysteries

If I'd saved all the Chinese food cartons I've ever had delivered and laid them side by side, I'm pretty sure they would reach from here to Shanghai. From the looks of things, my charge card should really be called Chinese Express:

12/04/87	MASTER WOK EAST	13.00
02/17/88	EMPIRE SZECHUAN PAVILION	61.25
11/19/88	FOO CHOW	35.45
01/17/89	1ST WOK	25.05
07/07/89	FOO CHOW	39.30
12/22/89	EMPIRE SZECHUAN PAVILION	14.94
01/12/90	TUNG SHING HOUSE	17.90
10/10/90	MASTER WOK II	16.90
10/11/90	MASTER WOK II	23.05
10/12/90	MASTER WOK II	10.25
01/05/91	MASTER WOK II	11.50
03/03/91	MASTER WOK EAST	17.70
05/28/91	CHEF 28	20.25
05/30/91	CHEF 28	9.30
09/15/91	CHEF 28	12.00
10/17/91	CHEF 28	12.25

I think single people have a special affinity for Chinese food
because it allows us to be noncommittal. Do I want something sweet or something sour? I can have both. Nobody
will demand that I be exclusive with the chicken or the
shrimp or the beef, because I can have them all, in one dish.

Date	Restaurant	Amount
01/01/93	COTTAGE EAST	10.75
04/26/93	MASTER WOK EAST	31.15
08/07/93	BILLY J NOODLES	26.25
09/04/93	BILLY J NOODLES	37.40
09/14/93	IMPERIAL DRAGON WEST	25.10
11/30/93	LAN TING EAST	15.70

And if I don't want to sit alone in a restaurant, they'll
deliver—so even though I've been told Mr. Right won't mag-
ically appear on my doorstep, with one call to Wan Fu, in
mere moments an entire Happy Family can come knocking.

Date	Restaurant	Amount
12/26/93	LAN TING EAST	14.95
01/04/94	LAN TING EAST	12.75
01/14/94	BILLY J NOODLES	17.25
02/01/94	LAN TING EAST	15.50
03/20/94	LAN TING EAST	11.75
03/30/94	LAN TING EAST	11.75

I do hear, though, that the Chinese food we eat in America is
not totally representative of what they eat over there, which
in some cases is not a loss. For instance, in some parts of
China, it's acceptable to eat cats and dogs. This could get
confusing because when your stomach growled, you wouldn't

know if it was because you were hungry or because your dinner was undercooked! On the upside, you'd have an airtight excuse if you were a kid in school: "I'm sorry, Mrs. Wang, but the dog ate my homework, and then my mom ate the dog."

04/17/94	HUNAN CITY	17.95
04/28/94	DRAGON WOK	25.05
05/11/94	IMPERIAL DRAGON WEST	23.50
05/23/94	LAN TING EAST	11.25
06/10/94	MASTER WOK EAST	23.60

As I further pondered the staggering number of charges for countless plates of chow mein, lo mein, and sweet and sour chicken, I came to a startling realization. Most of my charges were for dinners, some were for lunches, but none were for breakfast—and the truth is, while I could name ten or even twenty dishes that the Chinese have for other meals, I had *absolutely no idea* what they ate for breakfast. Just out of curiosity, I randomly called a dozen Chinese restaurants from the Manhattan phone book, and *not one of them* served breakfast. Surely they must have heard the same breakfast propaganda we have—that it's the most important meal of the day, that kids who skip breakfast are more likely to flunk their pop quizzes, drop out of school, and end up on death row. So what's the story here?

04/09/95	LAN TING EAST	11.75
09/11/95	BILLY J NOODLES	8.70
10/05/95	CITY NOODLE SHOP	27.25
12/02/95	LAN TING EAST	13.69

At the ad agencies where I've worked, Chinese food was practically the Official Food of Working Late. Could it be that the Chinese chefs are working so late making dinner for *other people* who are working late, that by the time they wake up it's lunchtime, and breakfast is no longer an issue? Or is there a whole Chinese breakfast tradition of which we non-Chinese folks are simply unaware—sweet and sour bacon, waffles foo yong, and General Tsao's Cream of Wheat?

10/26/96	IMPERIAL HUNAN	13.90
11/02/96	WALK N ROLL	25.65
11/10/96	IMPERIAL HUNAN	12.70
09/14/97	TWIN DRAGON CHINESE	8.12
09/19/97	EVERGREEN RSTR	7.25

Maybe the Chinese just aren't morning people, I theorized, a scenario that seems unlikely considering there's actually a Year of the Rooster, which is practically the poster bird for morning, yet there is no Year of the Owl or, for that matter, of any other nocturnal animal.

01/15/98	SPADES NOODLE	9.85
01/21/98	SPADES NOODLE	8.75
08/12/98	VEGA HOUSE	17.95

I've also noticed that of the hundreds of times I've had Chinese food delivered, not once has the delivery person been female. In this day and age, when women have taken bills to the Senate and rockets to the moon, how come they haven't made it to my apartment with some spareribs? Are the

restaurant owners afraid we can't handle the job emotionally? Do they think we'll be at an apartment door with the
food, whining, "Look, we need to talk. This is the second
time this month I've brought you your egg foo yong and I
just really need to know where this relationship is going?"
Are they afraid a woman will freak if she learns the pizza guy
was there the night before? "Look, I'm giving you an ultima-
tum," she'll say. "Either it's pizza or Chinese, but you can't
have both. Oh, and next time you want dinner on a Saturday
night, please have the courtesy to call by Wednesday!"

| 2/16/99 | VEGA HOUSE | 8.85 |
| 08/6/99 | CHINA FUN | 37.33 |

The Lazy/Busy Modern World

The advertising slogan for American Express used to be "Don't Leave Home Without It." But now that it's possible to use your Amex and have virtually anything you could ever want or need delivered right to your doorstep, their line might as well be "Don't Leave Home." I am much more of a hermit now than I've ever been, and, looking back over my charge bills, I can see just how the change happened.

Long before Blockbuster came to the neighborhood, my local video store was happy to deliver, and going to the movies required nothing more than going to the door to tip the guy:

07/06/91 VIDEO COUCH	SALES/RENTAL	32.48

Eventually, I could sit home and buy books, CDs, videos, and even a pasta maker.

11/25/98 AMAZON.COM	SUPERSTORE	32.97

I didn't even have to go out to find someone to go out with:

| 02/16/99 MATCHNET | MATCH.COM | 19.95 |
| 03/04/99 JDATE.COM | | 19.95 |

Little by little, modern life has left us starved for human contact. I'm afraid that next time I meet a guy I'm interested in and he asks for my number, I'll blurt out, "My home number is 555-5929, my work is 555-3020, my cell is 555-6641, my pager is 555-6640, my fax is 555-5399, my email is imsingle@yahoo.com. Or visit my website, www.amyneeds humancontact.com."

You'd think all this isolation would send people running out to a shrink's office, but that's not the case at all.

I just talked to Ellie, who's been feeling down lately, and she sounded momentarily relieved.

"Feeling better?" I asked.

"A little," she said. "I finally got my therapist to fit me in for a phone session."

A Few Notable Purchases

Before I say good-bye, I want to share some interesting tidbits I dredged up after reviewing a dozen years of my American Express bills.

Smallest Purchase Ever Charged:

08/28/98 GTE AIRFON	2 MINS	1.02

The most minuscule charge I ever had on my American Express was for a phone call I made from a plane, which I never would have expected since those calls are normally outrageously expensive. But the whole call lasted only two minutes, meaning I called my answering machine—as I do obsessively, several times a day—only to hear, "You have no new messages."

Even though I came up dry from the message well, the Jetsonian feeling of making a phone call from a plane was thrilling. I know I'll pass out from shock when, in another year or two, the inevitable happens: "Hello, Domino's? I'd like you to deliver a medium pizza with mushrooms and onions. My address is seat 25C, flight 1861, somewhere between Newark and Chicago. Just tell the guy to make a right at the fuzzy cloud, okay?"

Purchase I Couldn't Live Without:

03/17/96 DITRESSA SALON	HAIR CARE/PRODUCTS	59.28

I've been coloring my hair since I was in my twenties, when misguided strands of dental floss began popping up all over my head. By the time I got myself to my very first colorist, I was sure she'd take one look at me and offer me a senior discount. But maybe I'd blown my gray-hair problem out of proportion, because, I'm happy to report, she charged me full price.

In our youth-oriented culture, there's not much I need to explain about why I chose a good professional hair coloring as the one purchase I simply couldn't live without. Even gray-haired seniors don't want to admit to having gray hair, which is why products refer to their hair as silver, platinum, or some other high-end metal—come to think of it, I've never seen a conditioner meant "to enhance one's natural aluminum highlights" or to "give your hair the healthy shine of a brand-new tin can."

Purchase I Most Regret:

09/06/91 (NAME WITHHELD)	FLOOR COVERING	842.57

I don't fault this particular store, known in my area as one of the best places to shop for designer carpets and I'm sure deserving of the reputation. It was my own insane choice of an off-white color that proved to be completely impractical for someone who enjoys engaging in that popular activity known as living. It seemed that with each passing week, my off-white carpet became more "off" and less white, and it wasn't long before I found myself arranging my whole lifestyle around not wanting to soil it. I switched from serving red wine to white, bought slip-on shoes I could kick off the minute I walked through the door, and started making my coffee way weaker so I wouldn't spill it when caffeine-induced Parkinson's set in.

I don't want to sound mean-spirited and categorically indict white carpet, because though it wasn't right for me, it can be a beautiful choice for a single woman who never has red wine, cola, grape juice, coffee, tea, tomato sauce, gravy, barbecue sauce, or chocolate, and who never uses nail polish, foundation, lipstick, ballpoint pens, or shoes.

If you do happen to indulge in any of the above and own a white carpet, the plus side is that it will, after some years, display a rich and colorful history of your life. Recently I moved, and, once all my furniture was out of the apartment, I found a nostalgic collection of stains including a marinara blob from when Ed the Video Editor and I cooked pasta back in 1990, a nasty yellow circle from my friend Debbie's cat, and a dark patch from when my five-year-old neighbor lost control of his chocolate ice cream cone.

Don't worry, though—despite having so much personal history trapped in the stains of my old white carpet, I thus far have no plans to publish *Carpet Stains: True Tales of Life, Love, and Soy Sauce.*

Afterword

I do hope that you've enjoyed reading *Statements*. If you have a credit card charge for the book to look back on years later, maybe you'll even have a story about your purchase worth telling.

Looking ahead, for single women with a desire to be otherwise, I wish you all a future filled with the following charges:

MATCH.COM	−28.50 (CREDIT FOR CANCELLATION)	
KLEINFELD BRIDAL	VERA WANG	5,350.00
FOUR SEASONS RESORT	MAUI	2,949.67
BABY GAP	APPAREL	100.00
HARVARD UNIVERSITY	TUITION/BOOKS	32,500.00

Happy charging.

About the Author

Amy Borkowsky, a Manhattan-based comedian, is the creator of the popular *Amy's Answering Machine: Messages from Mom* CDs and author of the book by the same name. Previously, Amy was Executive Vice President and Creative Group Head at a major consumer advertising agency, where she won dozens of awards including five Clios, three Cannes Festival Lions, and an Emmy. Amy now devotes herself exclusively to performing, speaking, and developing new comedy projects. Visit her website at www.sendamy.com.